Contents

RECOVERING OUT LOUD

RECOVERING OUT LOUD

KRISTY HENDERSON

NEW DEGREE PRESS
COPYRIGHT © 2023 KRISTY HENDERSON
All rights reserved.

RECOVERING OUT LOUD
ISBN   979-8-88926-910-6 *Paperback*
            979-8-88926-911-3 *Ebook*

All names have been changed to protect the innocent (and the not-so-innocent).

To my husband,

For loving me enough for the both of us

until I learned to love myself.

YME, xoxo

Introduction

—

How long can you hold your breath? Thirty seconds? A minute?

Sitting quietly on my sofa as my husband makes dinner and my dog begs for scraps, I can hold my breath for forty-eight seconds.

Now imagine you're under water. How long can you hold your breath? Arms and legs pumping against the subtle current in its depths. Eyes immediately scanning for an escape. The CO_2 presses against the inside of your screaming lungs, warning signals fire in your brain.

What if something has trapped you from reaching the surface? Blocking out the light, bobbing slowly atop the intensifying waves. Fists pounding in slow motion on the lid of this watery coffin. I bet you could easily hold it for twenty, maybe thirty seconds longer.

I know because I did.

I held my breath just long enough to save myself not once, but twice. Most people think they would hear if someone was drowning by the sound of a scream or splash. In reality, it's often a silent death. By the time a person is drowning, they likely can no longer get their mouth above water to ask for help (Stop Drowning Now, n.d.).

In many ways, alcohol addiction is a muted, drowning death, too. One moment, you are floating through life, splashing and partying with your friends in the bright summer sun. The next moment, you have fallen in over your head and have no idea how you slipped into such depths. Flailing in panic and searching for salvation. Unable to find the words, the air you need, to call out for help. No clue of how long you have been inside your watery prison until time begins to run out and you have to make a choice: Accept your fate, or kick, flail, and fight until you get out.

No one ever sets out to become addicted to alcohol or drugs. No one is off daydreaming, "Life is so easy, maybe I'll get myself an addiction to make things more interesting." Yet for some, it comes on before we realize it and suddenly we're trapped under water desperate for a way out. Our only hope is we will be capable of asking for help before we run out of breath.

I never understood how terribly our society stigmatizes addictions to alcohol and drugs until I became addicted myself. We live in a society that punishes people for falling in, for becoming addicted. We even push away those who get sober, treat them as if they are «other," no longer fitting in with the rest of us. Addiction, such an undesirable distinction, is too ugly for common society. An open wound the sufferer is pressured to care for themselves by not burdening others with its gore. *Go fix yourself and stay far away from me.*

Rather than understanding that addiction is **not a moral failing, not a decision people make,** we cast them off to secretive meetings in church basements. We force them into prison cells or expensive treatment facilities to solve their problem on their own, chastising people who are already suffering far beyond what most can comprehend.

I used to be that way. I used to believe an alcoholic fit a certain mold or blueprint, suffered from an incurable disease. Broke, alone, unemployed with organ failure. I pictured brown paper bags and dirty hands, criminals and outcasts.

I had no idea they were just like everyone else until I became one of them.

* * *

I remember the summer my dad saved up and bought an above ground pool for our backyard. I stared at it from the kitchen window. The high midmorning sun danced off the water's surface like sparkling gems as I loaded another spoonful of Corn Pops into my mouth. It was the last Saturday in June, which meant my birthday party was soon to begin.

I was maybe six years old and bounced impatiently as I waited for the swimming to commence. Once the party was in full swing, Dad and his pals filled the pool from edge to edge with colorful floating rafts and chairs. Inflatable animals bobbed lazily on the surface like lily pads, begging me to jump in so my imagination could go on an adventure.

The kids all headed to the pool, claiming their inflatable perches as we formed a line at the base of the pool stairs. I waited anxiously until it was my turn to jump in and grinned when I spotted an open yellow floaty chair waiting for my arrival. I crawled over a few kids on blown-up chairs to get to it, then settled onto the supple plastic that was warmed by the summer sun. We floated and splashed as our parents mingled in the yard. I remember laughing and singing songs together at the top of our lungs, waving our arms and wiggling around on the slick wet surfaces of our tiny floating islands.

Then, without warning, I slipped off my banana-colored buoy and fell in.

I wasn't scared at first. My parents took me to swimming classes and I learned how to hold my breath diving for toys at the shallow end of the school's pool. Holding my breath, I swam back up toward the other kids excitedly, looking up at the underside of the floaties trying to locate my yellow perch.

Wait, which one is mine?

The chlorine in the pool began to sting my eyes as I looked up at the sea of inflatable rafts that split the sunlight into shards of light all around me. A fear rose within me, and I began pushing against the bottom of the pliable surfaces that sealed me inside the pool. I could hear the warbled laughter and splashing above me, but I had to puff my cheeks to stop my urge to scream for help.

I twisted, turned, looked for any opening back to fresh air while my struggle went unheard, unnoticed. I was surrounded by people yet completely alone in my battle.

My skinny legs kicked helplessly against the water, unable to touch the bottom of the three-foot-deep pool as I pushed against the plastic floaties above. Fear grew into panic as I fought the burn inside my lungs that was urgently screaming for air. I punched and prodded, searching for a way to penetrate the inflatable mass until I finally caught sight of the edge of the pool.

I used the last of the oxygen inside my lungs to fuel my graceless limbs as I scrambled for the blue wall. I snaked my little arm up between the wall and one of the inflated chairs, grabbed the hard plastic edge, and hoisted my body up through the narrow passage.

Dripping and gasping for air, I swept the mottled hair from my eyes and glanced around for acknowledgment of what I had just experienced. No one at the party was looking my way. Behind me, the kids continued to giggle and wiggle safely on their floaties, and the adults were off in the lawn enjoying each other's company. No one knew I was struggling. No one even realized the danger I faced.

I took a deep breath and folded myself over the edge with my legs still in the water and tried to get a grasp on what had just happened. I threw my legs over the pool rim one at a time and landed softly on the lawn below. Sprinting across the yard in my bare feet, I darted to my dad's side as he chatted with a friend. Tugging on the cuff of his shorts, I gasped as I pointed back at the pool, "I fell in and got stuck under everybody. I almost drowned!"

He looked over his shoulder at the pool. The sounds of silly children exploded with every splash of the water, the mist turning into a rainbow banner above the bobbing pool chairs. "Looks like you're fine now," he said with an encouraging pat on the back meant to usher me back toward the party.

I stood frozen for a moment, following his gaze back to the pool. The swimmers kept swimming, parents kept drinking and talking, kids chased each other on bikes through the yard. Everything proceeded as if nothing had happened at all. Even though the danger was gone, the fear refused to leave.

If adult life was like the pool, I was partying on my pink flamingo floaty chair with sunlight in my eyes. Sweet drinks and loud laughs filled the party, and everything was going swimmingly. It wasn't until my mid-thirties I found myself drowning again, this time in boxed wine and hoppy IPAs. I lived my life like a never-ending party, filling my cup like everyone else and horsing around on pumped-up pool toys. By the time I realized I was in trouble, I had already fallen in over my head. I had actually been treading water for years. I found myself faced with my own mortality, kicking and punching against the force that held me underwater. Struggling to keep on living. Scraping to find a way to survive.

I don't know which sip did me in or how long I was under before I realized I was in danger. I got addicted to alcohol even though I wasn't an "alcoholic." My parents weren't either. The term «alcoholic" is no longer even recognized by the medical community, having been replaced with the term "alcohol use disorder" or AUD. It is defined as an "impaired ability to stop or control alcohol use despite adverse social, occupational, or health consequences" (NIAAA 2020). I had become addicted to an addictive substance. But recovery wouldn't come so easily.

When it came to getting sober, I'd have to drag myself up to the surface for air time and time again. I quit drinking multiple times but struggled to find a sober life that would last. After being told to "keep drinking" while seeking help through AA, I tried to reconcile if I was even worthy of recovering. I had to test my capabilities to see if I had the power to pull myself to dry land. It wasn't until I learned the importance of doing it *out loud* that I found a way to recover once and for all.

As addicts, we often tread water and struggle in silence, proving to the imaginary judges in life that we are strong and resilient and can do it on our own. We bottle the fear and the anguish together inside to prove we are happy and successful in life. We hide the broken parts that make us undeserving of love, connection, and joy. We can kick until we're too tired to stop the sinking, slowly disappearing into the dark, cold depths below. Or we can teach each other to swim. We can clear the path to the exits and offer a hand when someone falls in. That's why I recover out loud.

I recover out loud because suffering alone in the privacy of my own mind was slowly destroying me. Hiding the parts of me I thought were damaged and unworthy crippled me from being able to share the rest of myself with the people I loved. Alcohol blurred the lines until I could no longer tell where I began and the person I pretended to be ended.

I recover out loud to hold the light for those still hiding in shadows.

I recover out loud to share hope for those with none.

To share the joy I've found from facing my own personal demons and winning.

To share love I hope you learn to hold for yourself.

I recover out loud to help break the stigmas that keep addiction and mental health taboo. How can we ever expect people to feel safe in our society if we don't provide a refuge to turn to when they are in trouble? I dream that we will treat people struggling with addiction with the kindness this level of anguish requires, and stop branding them as outcasts and treating them as such.

I have watched friends drowning in their own addictions but never knew how to offer them a hand. I'd watch from afar as the people I loved found their way ashore, toweling themselves off on their own. But oddly, once they began living a sober life, I struggled to look them in the eye. I was so busy worrying they could see right through me, see me for the addiction I hid. I was too ashamed to sympathize with what they must have gone through.

Not everyone was so lucky. It's for people like them, the ones who couldn't save themselves. Who couldn't shout for help. Those are the ones I recover out loud for. I would have given anything to get out of the pool sooner.

But the interesting part about addiction was learning it wasn't just about absence of drinking. Just staying out of the pool, away from a drink or avoiding a party, wasn't the final answer. True recovery meant understanding why I drank in the first place and having to decide once and for all if that was who I truly wanted to be. If I was going to make a full recovery and reclaim myself, I'd have to understand why I fell overboard in the first place.

Or risk drowning once again.

The Sentence

—

You are not going to live to see your fortieth birthday, Kristy.

The words hit me unexpectedly and I stood frozen in place. Captive. Stunned by the impact of each word's blow. I heard them repeating in my mind as the words floated around slowly inside my head. Everything around me melted away. Had it not been for the flash of the stage lights I would have believed I was dreaming.

The darkness of the old auditorium was so thick I could barely see my husband and friends standing directly in front of me. Music swelled and rose to the ceiling high above, commanding the attention of everything it bounced off. The air inside the room felt drawn to the stage. It was as if a rope was tethered to the very breath that filled my lungs, pulling forcefully against my chest.

Tonight was supposed to be just a regular night out. Friends, drinks, live music, and belly laughs. I don't know why things changed or how it all went wrong because that is not how it panned out.

Sometimes I can still taste the tears. Still feel their burning heat as they streamed down my face that night. The saltiness seared into my soul.

* * *

My husband Mitch and I drove to downtown Saint Paul to meet four of our friends for dinner and a concert. It was a gorgeous, fall day in Minnesota with soft, passing clouds that floated by in a lazy river of bright blue sky. I peered silently out the passenger window while he drove, admiring the changing colors of the leaves and smell of autumn in the air as I tried to lighten my attitude. A thrum of activity buzzed about the crowds as we drove around searching for a place to park, cool wind whipping my hair across my face.

I wanted to be excited, giddy, and grinning from ear to ear. I did. But lately it felt like that level of happiness was somehow out of reach. As if it was no longer in the assortment of emotions I could choose from. Discontinued. Rubbish. *Sorry, kid. That life isn't for you anymore.* Life felt as though it was reduced to a constant state of anxiety and chaos while everyone around me seemed to have it all together. Me, I was just trying to wrangle up all the pieces of my life into a bag tight to my chest. But the threads were wearing thin and threatening to fall apart. The only thing I could do was smile and pretend everything was okay.

So I smiled. I smiled and pretended because that was how I learned to survive many years before.

We met our friends at a popular new bratwurst joint, flush with dozens of specialty beers on tap to start the night off properly. It was barely five o'clock, but I had already helped myself to a midday beer or two and a couple glasses of wine before we went out for the night. I didn't even feel a buzz. I rarely did anymore. At this point, it took two drinks just to feel normal.

The food was as delicious as it was hyped up to be and we finished a couple pints before closing our tab and heading the few blocks to the theater on foot. I pulled my long sleeves down over my hands to warm them, chilled and shaking after clutching the frosted glasses at the restaurant during dinner. Crisp air swirled between the buildings as we strolled to the venue and the six of us shared stories along the way.

My best friend, Madeline, walked next to me, and we joked playfully about silly things that had happened in the weeks since last we saw each other. I entertained her with my bloody antics as a clumsy mountain biker and she laughed knowingly at the ridiculous medical supply bill at the pharmacy after. We exchanged new tidbits of knowledge, life hacks, and hot spots to check out. Crafty new uses for duct tape, the new music venue in town, and fancy new breweries to check out. She was the type of friend that every time we were together it was easy and relaxed. We talked like we hadn't seen each other in ages but with the comfort and closeness of what I imagine growing up with sisters must feel like.

Even though Madeline and I were close, I still never let on about the numbness I was feeling. Not with her, not Mitch, no one. For years, I experienced anxiety and depression which worsened as time went on. What I believed was rooted in work stress and insecurity was growing, spreading over the full expanse of my life. Each low was descending lower and each high evaporated into a dull haze. Nothing of me remained but an echo of who I had once been, going through the motions and pretending like everything was under control.

We smiled and laughed straight up the steps and into the main doors of the historic Roy Wilkins Auditorium. We arrived shortly before Royal Blood was to open for Queens of the Stone Age (QotSA), so we ordered a round at the bar and eyed up the crowded music hall. With a tall beer in hand, I followed the group onto the main floor as we made our way to the edge of the crowd. The bodies were packed tight, so we stayed on the outer edge mere feet from the back wall.

The openers were electric, coming at us with so much raw power and feral energy that we each looked at each other in utter astonishment. We exchanged glances and mouthed our praise to one another, "Holy, shit! They're awesome!" Our eyes were wide with surprised grins reflecting the flash of stage lights. There were only two people on stage, but they filled the room with a magnetic sound like an orchestra jacked up on Red Bull playing Led Zeppelin tunes.

I bobbed my head, swayed, and rocked along to the beat, but it felt like a layer was missing. I could hear the music but was unable to connect with it like I once had years ago. A small ache throbbed inside me as I noticed the void. I felt like a robot. I could *feel* the vibrations of the bass drum penetrate my chest and rattle my heart. I could stomp out the rhythm with my feet on autopilot. I could even sing along to the one song I knew, but the passion they poured into their songs fell at my feet as if sung in a foreign language. It was the same hollow space I felt between myself and everyone I loved.

They finished their set and left the audience charged with the energy they exploded on stage. We grabbed some more beers at the bar while the stagehands swapped out the equipment for the headliner's arrival. "Can you believe that?" "That was amazing!" The six of us were awestruck, grasping for words to describe the powerful storm we'd just witnessed. You could tell they were hungry, chasing hard after their dreams and creating a frenzied path for themselves without looking back. The intensity was electric, leaving the entire room amplified with frenetic excitement.

As QotSA walked out on stage, the lights dimmed and quickly faded to black, leaving us in complete darkness. The entire room was blanketed in blackness except for a dozen thin pillars of light on stage that lit up and wobbled on rounded bases. They swayed gently from side to side like a buoy in the ocean. Lead singer, Josh Homme, lumbered to the front center of the stage, his tall, slender stature looming above the rhythmic lights. Undulating like muted metronomes, the lights drew me in like a moth to flame. As he began plucking out the first notes on his electric guitar, I knew they were opening with the song "If I Had a Tail." The drummer stomped the kick drum, and all eyes were on the stage.

That's when everything changed.

The stage lights went black. The back of the auditorium where we stood was submerged in darkness so thick, I suddenly felt like I was the only one there. A feeling of unease washed over me. I stepped forward to stand just behind Mitch's shoulder, resting my hand on his back to signal to him I was there and reassure myself I wasn't alone. As the pillars lit back up and voices filled the air, I hid from the last slivers of light trying to understand the churning feelings inside.

I peered between the faint silhouettes of the other concert goers as the feeling of foreboding grew. My eyes were glued to the singer as he opened his mouth, his voice masculine, feral, captivating. There was an edge of darkness over the slow-rising desert rock number, resetting the energy in the theater to make room for their own crescendo of sound. Something about the words were different, as if I was hearing them for the first time. My lips formed the words along with Homme, singing about the raw honesty of tears. The presence of them, good or bad, from pain or pleasure, the way they trail down our cheeks exactly the same. Like an arrow through my heart, the verse landed on the bullseye of a pain I had denied carrying for too long.

As if called by the words rising out of his chest, tears pooled atop the lower lids of my eyes and blurred the wobbling tubes into smears of light before me. Like big, fat summer rain drops, they crested over my lashes and dove thoughtlessly onto my cheeks below.

It came on so suddenly, I couldn't stop the tears from falling and I scrambled through my mind to find an explanation. As the song continued, I could sense the sadness building deep inside me. I clenched a fist tightly and pressed it to the center of my chest. It was a futile attempt, as if my hand's proximity to my beating heart could help me soothe the pain I held inside. The blackness in the room camouflaged me from the eyes of strangers while the lights danced off the tears washing over my face.

The songs kept coming and the tears refused to slow. Every now and then, I would place my hand tenderly between Mitch's shoulder blades to reassure him of my presence in the void. Secretly saying a prayer to the universe that he wouldn't turn around. *What is this?* I asked myself frantically. *Where is this coming from? Why the hell won't it stop?*

There, in the shadows, I was overcome with a knowing, an understanding so real it was as if my heart was speaking directly to me.

You are not going to live to see your fortieth birthday, Kristy.

A guitar solo on stage drew cheers from the crowd and I stood motionless. Tears fell from my eyes as I struggled to take a deep breath.

I was only thirty-seven years old that night but deep down inside the words were undeniable. It was a brutally honest slap in the face and the only one to blame for getting to this point was me. I hadn't felt something so honest, heard a sentence so true, for over a decade. Not since the day I realized my husband would be in my life forever. How I knew it before he ever asked me out. It was the one voice I trusted the most.

I first met Mitch when I walked into his bicycle shop on a Thursday afternoon, on a mission to purchase my first bike as an adult. It was late summer, just a few months after my twenty-sixth birthday. I was back living with my dad and stepmom after breaking off a three-year relationship and three years of sobriety. I was obsessed with the movie *Under the Tuscan Sun* with Diane Lane at the time. Intrigued by the way she was able to recover from heartbreak. Inspired by the new life she built. It was time for me to do the same.

My plan was to buy a bike and book a wine tour in Italy as a gift to myself. A fresh start after a hard time in my life. I met with Mitch a few times at the shop so he could customize the bike perfectly for me. After each sizing session, we would talk about music and hobbies, sharing honest nuggets of myself to a stranger who was helping fulfill a dream. As he prepared to negotiate the final price of the bike with all the bells and whistles, I laughed and smiled. "Hey, I get it. It's a full package. An investment." I amused him with tales of my greatest fishing follies and love of the outdoors. My answer had surprised him, and he laughed, giving me a discount anyway.

Mitch sold me a lovely road bike and gave me his number before I walked out the door. "Call me if you ever need a friend to ride with." I didn't have any close friends who rode bikes back then so on sunny weekends I would call up Mitch and ask if he was free to go for a spin.

After a few rides and long, effortless discussions, Mitch invited me to come watch him race and hang out with his friends one Sunday afternoon. The race was captivating and full of drama as local athletes took to the off-road course. Afterward, we headed into downtown Minneapolis to hang out with his friends on a loading dock behind a friend's bike shop. Fifty or so people ambled around with beers in their hands and smiles on their faces as they greeted and laughed with one another.

I sat on the edge of the dock, talking to two of Mitch's friends who wanted to know what got me interested in bikes. I was swimming in awe at the crew of people around and bashfully told them of the whim I had to venture off to Italy. I looked over my shoulder to where Mitch sat with an old friend on a bench, casually basking in the sun with a view of all the fun.

Our eyes locked and time paused for an instant. The depths of the chocolate tones in his eyes were rich and tender, welcoming me to hold his gaze a moment longer. Everything in my peripheral blended together in a mash of white noise and swirls of color. I took a deep breath and, in that second, was flush with warmth and light down to my toes. It wasn't spelled out over his head like a marquee, but my heart filled with a knowing that he would be in my life forever.

A simple imprint on my soul. And I knew.

It made it quite easy to say, "Yes," hours later when he finally stumbled through his words and asked me out on a date. Shy and innocent, we giggled together in anticipation of seeing each other again. Less than two years later, we'd turn my "yes" into our "I do."

To me, I think of the knowing as my inner voice, my soul. That place inside still connected to some universal understanding beyond all that I can imagine. The one in my life that whispered "Run!" whenever danger stepped out of the shadows or sat in peaceful silence as I gazed up at shooting stars on clear nights. My inner voice, the final guiding light at the end of every storm I have endured.

As the concert continued, my husband and friends remained unaware of my internal undoing. Delicate trails of tears had widened into broad strokes that washed across my cheeks. As the blurred lights danced in my vision, waves of memories rolled up and through me, my feet and legs holding me in place like an anchor as I tried to withstand the force of them all.

Countless mornings waking up with hangovers flashed before me. Each daybreak spent scrambling to piece together my behavior after another blackout. Late night arguments with Mitch. Bottled up tension and fears I couldn't name. Stumbles and mistakes, shortcomings and failures, played on as each song transition passed me by.

Mixed with each song came painful memories of hateful self-talk that trumpeted in the start of every day. Horrible, cruel thoughts burned bright in my mind as I struggled to get myself out of bed.

How much did you drink last night? You loser. What's wrong with you? Idiot. Failure. I bet he's pissed at you. No one likes you. Stupid. They don't care. He's better off without you. You'll never get that job. They hate you. Why can't you do anything right? You're a drunk. This is your life. You don't get to be happy.

No one would even miss you if you were gone.

Each morning, I stepped into the boxing match inside my head and took blow after blow without ever putting up my gloves. Throwing punches and slowly destroying myself piece by piece. I'd make coffee and hate myself. Sit down at my desk at the office and feel like an imposter. I would stare at my phone worried that Mitch was somewhere planning to leave me on the other end. I was so focused on surviving the onslaught, I could barely concentrate on anything else.

I felt disconnected from the people I loved, living in constant fear that one day they would all leave. I was paranoid Mitch and my friends were planning interventions and tough conversations. Each new song that began carried in new waves of painful revelations and more questions I couldn't answer.

How did I get here? How did it all go so wrong?

I had become so dependent on alcohol to deal with every aspect of my life. Bouncing between boxed wine and blackouts, I was trapped inside my own stone walls constructed to shield me from pain. I covered my insecurities with shots and wild behavior. I drowned my sadness and agony by filling goblets with merlot, fueled my anger with hard liquor, and tried to construct a perfect persona with towers of empty beer cans. No matter how much I drank, it never took away the stress of the day, never eased the tensions of uncomfortable relationships or made me a better friend. It didn't make me a better spouse or do a damn thing to care for myself.

I had everything I could dream of in my life. A loving partner, sweet dog, and safe home. I had family and friends who cared for me. But I drank like I was trying to purge it all away.

I was already dead inside. It was as though I was living in the shadow of who I really was, only pretending to be the person I was expected to be. I was hollow and empty, a small flicker of life still inhabiting the vacant space of my own human form. It was exhausting, and for the first time, I started to recognize it.

The waves crashed against me as I stood motionlessly in the crowd, no longer caring about who saw me coming apart in the lights that passed over my face. Like a statue, I rode out the storm, taking it all in like gospel without questioning a feeling that passed through me. If my husband looked back in search of me, I'd bury my face in his arm endearingly. I'd distract him with a squeeze to keep him from seeing defeat in my swollen eyes.

My life was nothing like what I understood alcoholism to look like. I wasn't raised by addicts or alcoholics. I was raised by two parents who loved and cared for me to the ends of the earth. I was educated and successful. I married a man who cherished and doted on me unconditionally. I had friends and family, a safe home, and an active life outdoors. I began tasting the bitter agony of losing it all.

I didn't even fear it. The only thing that rose to frighten me there in the void was how willingly I accepted the truth as it set in.

You are going to drink yourself to death, Kristy. Yes, it seemed fitting. *I probably will.* I could recognize my own self-destruction as if looking back on my loved ones who succumbed to alcohol before me. Those who took early graves and left seas of people in mourning long after they were gone. Somewhere, deep down inside, that small voice spoke in the moments between breaths, calling to me. I wasn't going to live to see forty. This was my life. My truth. And alcohol was going to ferry me to my grave.

As the final song played, I took five slow metered breaths and wiped at the tears. The soaked cuffs of my sleeves were wadded in my hands like a child trying to pull herself together. My eyes were still glossy and red as the lights turned up but, thanks to alcohol, that was nothing out of the norm.

With my practiced smile, I followed my crew out of the theater and nodded along as my husband and friends recounted how phenomenal the show was. I never told them a word about what I had just gone through. *How could I? What would I say?*

Some people believe addiction is a death sentence. A diagnosis leading to a lifetime of withdrawal and longing for a substance or experience you must never encounter again. A plague not to be spoken of, a secret only to be shared in the privacy of hidden rooms with metal chairs and stale coffee. Lesser known, unfortunately, are those brave enough to speak about addiction openly. Those souls who had fallen to the darkest depths of their existence and found the strength within themselves enough to say, "This is not how my story ends."

Dr. Gabor Maté, author, physician, and addiction expert, wrote in *In the Realm of Hungry Ghosts*, "Not all addictions are rooted in abuse or trauma, but I do believe they can all be traced to painful experience. A hurt is at the center of *all* addictive behavior" (Maté 2020). His research and experience with addiction is intimate in the way it examines the human experience. His explanations seek to remove the stigmas that surround it so you can look directly into the heart of the beast that rages within those trapped in addiction. If only I had found his research earlier, maybe I could have made a change that night. Maybe I could have stopped the fall.

As we walked back to our car that night, the air felt painfully thin, and I forced myself to breathe while those words kept replaying in the back of my head. I felt separated from my body as if I was watching everything through a camera. The conversation unfolded in slow motion while my mind was miles away.

I tried to imagine a future for myself to prove they weren't true, but all I could envision was darkness. I smiled and hugged our friends goodbye as we walked to our cars, then climbed into the passenger seat so Mitch could drive us home. The radio played in the background to fill the silence in the cab. Words floated from my mind down into my chest, constricting my breath and stealing my focus. I gazed out the window at my own reflection in the side mirror half expecting to see a death sentence branded across my forehead for all to see.

Dead woman walking.

Woodlake Lodge

———

I was only fourteen years old when I ordered my first drink at a bar. A sweet, lime-flavored frozen margarita with an umbrella was delivered to the table and placed in front of me. "Enjoy," the server said as she smiled at me with a wink before walking away.

I was surprised to learn it was legal in Wisconsin to drink underage in a bar if accompanied by an adult. Any adult. No questions asked. At a time in my life where I was struggling to figure out how I fit in, it was a very welcome surprise.

I was spending another summer weekend in the north woods of Wisconsin with my best friend, Jenny, and her family of five at their lakeside cabin getaway. Our friend, Stella, was also along for another adventure weekend of swimming, bonfires, s'mores, and the *legendary* snipe hunting. I felt so lucky to get invited to go to the cabin with them multiple times each summer. Some of my greatest memories took place playing under the trees of the expansive Chequamegon-Nicolet National Forest and swimming in the clear waters of Lake Namekagon.

Jenny's mom started up their pontoon boat one afternoon to take us kids over to a nearby resort to play pinball and pool in their game room. Jenny, Stella, and I waited impatiently on the dock for Jacki and Jeff, Jenny's two younger siblings, to gather up their allowance so we could leave. They were only two and three years younger than us respectively, and we did almost everything together at the lake. We laughed as we watched them running clumsily down to the dock, dragging their life jackets behind as they made their way down the sloped lawn. Their dad waved from the cabin deck as we pulled away, staying back to fix something adults fix.

We followed Jenny's mom through the rustic entryway and straight into the bar. It had a mezzanine level with pool tables and arcade games that overlooked the tavern tables below. A long staircase of thickly lacquered logs curved dramatically along the outskirts of the room to join the two spaces.

The five of us kids ran up the stairs excitedly to check out what games were available and found a group of boys near our age already making sloppy work of a game of pool. Jenny, Jacki, and Stella immediately perked up at the sight of the young boys. My friends were voluptuous, curvy, and had an inkling of the power their own bodies held. I was a shapeless tomboy who liked to go fishing or scale trees with sturdy limbs to lounge on. Those types of interests kept me in the crowd when I was younger, but I was starting to realize it no longer helped me fit in the same way. Jeff and I rolled our eyes annoyedly to one another and made our way back down to his mom sitting alone at a table near the bar.

"What are you two doing down here?" she asked as we sat down next to her.

"They're just flirting with boys," I replied as I nodded toward the balcony above, completely disinterested in the new social ritual.

Jeff asked his mom for some quarters then ran back upstairs with his new haul, past the pool table and straight to a pinball game in the corner to play alone. I stayed in the seat and watched my friends through the wooden railing.

"Well, do you like margaritas?"

I hadn't realized I was far off in thought until Jenny's mom, Lily, interrupted my silence with the unexpected question. I felt like time stood still as I blinked at her and replayed the question again in my head, trying to understand what she was asking me. "What do they taste like?" I asked, and Lily took a long drag on her cigarette as the corners of her mouth curled into a playful smile.

* * *

Growing up, I was the only child in a single-parent home, my parents separating before I turned two years old. They each loved me deeply but didn't know how to extend that same tenderness and adoration for one another, so they shared custody of me while my primary home was with Dad. His house was a half hour outside the cities in a quaint suburban town with a Lutheran church in every neighborhood, the only establishments to outnumber the bars. Until high school,

I was the only child of divorced parents in any of my classes, and it molded more of me than I ever understood at the time.

We lived in the corner house on a dead-end road on a gorgeously wooded street. Half of the families had kids around my age, and we played from sunup to sundown every summer without ever leaving the block. We built tree forts and trails in our yards together, raced bikes, and searched for wildlife. I can't imagine growing up anywhere better.

My dad was the maintenance supervisor for a family-owned lumber yard and picked up odd jobs occasionally to make sure we had enough to live a comfortable life. I was a straight-A student who did my homework as soon as I got home so I could go outside and play. If I wasn't on a bike or in a tree, I was cuddled up with a teddy bear and the latest *Nancy Drew* mystery I got for my birthday.

Mom was a nurse manager at the regional treatment center and lived half an hour from us. She eventually remarried before I turned eight and had twins, a boy and girl. Something about her second husband made me apprehensive, even at a young age. It wasn't until I got older that I finally realized how important gut instincts were.

I used to spend a few weekends each month at Mom's house but it was around this time that my invites got fewer and farther between. "Something came up," my dad would say as he hung the olive green phone back on its cradle on the kitchen wall and turned to tell me I wasn't going to see my mom that day. What he never explained was how my mom was clawing her way out of an abusive marriage. He never told me she wanted to keep me away from the escalating violent behavior of a man she had trusted and started a new family with.

My dad couldn't have told me. I was too young and innocent to understand what was happening. I didn't realize her husband's drunken, midnight tirades were just a taste of what living with him truly was like. When I would visit, my mom would sleep in the bedroom with my younger siblings and me, shielding us from his anger when he was drunk. I remember him storming into the bedroom in the middle of the night. His tall, intimidating figure blocked out the hallway light as he bellowed into the darkness while we cowered together. Furious, he stood there demanding to know where the bottles of Jim Beam were hidden and commanding her to give him money for drugs.

When Mom no longer seemed to want me to visit, I didn't realize it was about him. How could I? But the more my parents shielded me from the hostage situation Mom was trapped in, the more I started to think she just didn't love me anymore. I didn't know if it was something I did or something I was never going to be. It wasn't until my early forties while watching the first weeks of Russia's attack on Ukraine in 2022 that I finally started to understand why I was kept at arm's length.

I remember watching the national broadcast one night as Ukrainian soldiers were shown evacuating elderly citizens, women, and children to neighboring countries for safety. The tragic images of families fleeing their homes with just the clothes on their back played out in front of me. I watched as the broadcast narrowed in on a little girl with curly blonde hair and a small teddy bear in her hand. Her mother held her other hand as they crossed the wire fence border to safety. *The soldiers need to get them out so they can focus on the war. She got me out so she could fight. So she had one less child in danger.*

Like me, that little girl probably didn't understand the turmoil around her. Somewhere in the silence between Dad's vague explanations left room for my interpretations to veer far from the truth. No one could tell me what I did wrong or how I could fix it. My parents didn't have to stay together and my connection to my mother was fading. I started to believe I was the problem. It was me that was broken and unlovable. I started to believe they could each leave me at any time, and I was wrapped in panic not knowing how I could prevent it.

I had it so wrong back then, and the agony of it broke my foundation to pieces.

* * *

Lily smiled from across the table and leaned back in her chair. "They're sweet. They taste like lime, you'll love it." The waitress returned and Lily ordered us frozen margaritas, leaning in close to explain how adults are allowed to order kids a drink in Wisconsin. "They don't know you're not my daughter," she winked and I relaxed back into my chair.

For her, it was probably a light-hearted way to make me feel less alone at the resort. For me, hanging out one on one with Jenny's mom was a connection I hadn't realized I was longing for. It's funny which issues we choose to plant our foot on. Even though I was a perfectionist kid who wanted everyone to be happy and like me, I had the wherewithal to put my foot down when it came to boys. Back then, I felt safer admitting I still thought boys were "gross" than I ever felt admitting I longed for time with my mom.

Hanging out with Lily often made me think of Mom. Both of them smiled with wide, Cheshire grins that pulled you into their joy unknowingly. When my mom laughed, her whole body would bounce as she sucked in air between laughs, her arms and legs emphasizing how funny the moment was. Lily did, too. It had been years since I saw my mom laugh like that. That beautiful smile, a memory of my mom feeling that free, was starting to fade away like old Polaroids of us from long ago. Lily's smile was a surrogate that I leaned on.

The waitress returned with our drinks, and I played with the yellow umbrella as I took my first sip. Sweet chunks of icy liquid pulled up the straw and into my mouth. Lily and I looked at each other with goofy, smiling duck faces as we sipped away slowly, trying to avoid getting brain-freezes and chatted about fireworks and pontoon cruises yet to come for the day.

After a while, the rest of the girls got curious about our gig-gles, or maybe the boys got called away. Either way, they returned inquisitive about what we were up to. Lily filled them in on the tastiness of our frozen treats, waving a circle around the table as she ordered more for the girls so they'd join us. As they sipped their drinks and smiled, giggling about brain-freezes and pinching the bridge of their nose, I sat and took it all in. We were all together, having the time of our lives.

Addictive drugs and alcohol work by causing a sudden release of dopamine in our brain, triggering the body's reward system to fire in anticipation. Food can raise dopamine levels and develop reinforcing attachments through its pleasurable flavors and textures. Alcohol, with its sweet liqueurs and smooth wines, is also capable of activating the reward system by way of taste. But that's only the first way it triggers the reward network.

Research has found that alcohol activates two peaks in the dopamine system. First, with the delicious liquid that slides down your throat. Second, when it crosses the blood-brain barrier, something no chocolate, coffee, sex, nor exercise can do. The results showed the "alcohol-associated stimuli acquire an abnormal emotional and motivational significance that results in excessive control over the drinker's behavior. This excessive control constitutes the essence of addiction" (Di Chiara 1997).

I wasn't born addicted to alcohol, but my fear of abandonment turned me into a people-pleasing perfectionist. I tried to win love through achievements and strived to make everyone else happy as a validation of my worth. Ensure everyone liked me. At the cabin or the lodge, we were smiling and laughing together like a family. It was the false reality I attached to that drink which became my obsession.

Drinking intertwined itself with the summer nights at the cabin, twisting in the cool evening breeze with the giggling and squeals of children at play. Echoes bouncing off the still black lake. In the darkness, alcohol became my lantern. A guiding light.

A blaze orange, double-teaming dopamine oasis to venture off to time and time again.

* * *

Drinking alcohol at Jenny's cabin became a parallel life, a secret to keep from my own parents and a strong bond between me and my friends. Her parents would make large pitchers of "thunder punch," which I could only guess was some mix of Malibu, rum, and fruity mixers that we would all sip on as we trolled along the lake on their pontoon. We would be out on the water for hours, tubing, stopping to swim in the bays or have a light lunch. On the deck, we would spray lemon juice in our hair to try and lighten it to a more summery tone. It was a fun departure from my typical, mousy blonde shade.

My cheeks would flush, and my smile stretched wider than I could control. I'd feel a warmth in my belly and reveled when it seemed the afternoon sun formed another dimension, almost palpable as we glided along the lake.

Back on land, us kids would roam free for hours on end at the cabin, running through the woods, exploring the bay on jet skis, or walking into the small north wood's town. One day, we walked into the little country store down the dirt road from her cabin where we often took our allowance so we could buy a candy bar or soda. This time, as the five of us walked up and down the aisles looking for treats, I saw the racks of alcohol bottles on the far wall and wandered silently over to it. Walking slowly down the aisle, I took in their labels, the different color liquids that filled them, and saw an opportunity form before me.

If more As can make Dad proud of me, more alcohol will make things more fun, right?

As Jenny and Stella bought a candy bar each, I swiftly grabbed a small bottle of vodka that resembled the one at the cabin and a bottle of sour apple Schnapps. The bright green liquid fired up my imagination and my taste buds in anticipation of how sweet it must taste. I crammed them quietly down the front of my shorts as Jacki turned the corner and caught me in the act.

Her eyes glinted and the grin that stretched across her face was wickedly mischievous as she took in my hunched form, trying to hide the shape of the bottles under the hem of my shirt. I hesitantly smiled back at her and breathed a sigh of relief she seemed to approve. I pulled my shirt down as far as it would give and we moved quickly to follow our friends out the door, waving to the clerk as we stepped outside and took a huge breath. Jacki and I giggled as I tried to silence the glass bottles that clanged together in my shorts until we were far enough away from the store to brag about our loot.

Our friends were mildly upset but it didn't stop anyone from taking pulls off the bottles later that night. We snuck away from the adults after dusk and stowed away to the loft above the garage. With music playing and a stack of board games to enjoy, we passed around the bottles, drunk and singling loudly to every song we knew.

Jeff went to bed and Jenny and Stella finally had enough. They wanted to go to sleep but Jacki and I were still climbing along on our drunken adventure reluctant to end all the fun. We passed each bottle back and forth until they went dry, laughing and high-fiving as our annoyed friends wandered off to bed. "They just don't get it," was slurred. *Hiccup.*

I woke up the next morning with a terrible headache. I could hear Stella and Jenny in the kitchen talking as I rolled away from the bright sunlight charging through the thin linen curtains, a foul taste in my mouth. Before I could make sense of everything I was feeling, Jacki burst into the room and barreled straight for the bathroom door next to my bed. As the loud echo of her howls into the toilet bowl grew louder, so did the laughter from the kitchen. From everyone... her mom, dad, siblings, friend.

As my stomach lining began dancing to its own rhythm in reply, I rolled back over and pulled the pillow over my head.

* * *

In a study conducted at a New England university, researchers found that female students with lower self-esteem drank more alcohol to conform or fit in than their more confident counterparts. Their findings supported multiple theories which looked into the innate human need to belong and how self-esteem directly correlates with how well we perceive our acceptance by others (Schick, Nalven, Spillane 2022).

Self-esteem is the gauge by which we measure our own ability to connect to the people in our lives. But, like all skills and abilities we may have, not all of them are accurate or honed in. Some skills need work. For me, my self-esteem was fragile from the beginning, and it broke before I ever got to junior high. But I hadn't waited until college to find alcohol as my key to fitting in. No, I was barely a teenager when I attempted to fill the holes in my self-esteem with fruity cocktails and cheap vodka. Sadly, what began as a small act of rebellion became a false narrative which would take decades to unlearn.

Fast forward to my early thirties. My husband, Mitch, and I were at an outdoor wedding for a pair of his close friends. The wedding and reception took place under huge, old trees at the bride's parents' home but to say it was a backyard wedding was to sell it way too short. The property and home felt more like we were in the heart of a vineyard with stunning landscaping and Italian wedding lights strung through the trees. Opulent, white-clothed tables and chairs were assembled under the high-society tent and floor-to-ceiling windows on the house glowed with orange light as the evening sun faded.

The ceremony was lovely, and I tried not to cry too many happy tears as I held tightly to my husband's hand. He knew a lot of attendees from his years of bicycle racing, but I was still new to the scene and trying to get to know them. As we ate our dinner and I listened to them retell bike racing stories, we started to hear whispers of an impending storm. The whispers soon turned into more urgent conversation as I noticed the eldest members of the family being led into the house.

A tornado was heading our way.

We stood to the side and watched as the remaining elders and bridal party were led into the house, then jumped in line with the rest of the guests. With only a salad in our stomachs, our group of friends nestled ourselves onto soft couches and chairs in the basement family room of their home.

As the tornado sirens howled off in the distance, the parents and bridal party started lining all the tables and flat surfaces with the contents that once filled the tent's open bar. In moments, we had gone from the candle-lit tent at sunset to a brightly lit room, buzzing with an undertone of fear. Anxiety set in for me and I was trying to get comfortable in the confined space, finding my only relief by refilling my glass of wine over and over and over. The woman who sat across the coffee table from me had given off an air of annoyance toward me since I met her. I kept my glass full to try to muffle my own self-conscious thoughts.

I worried the rest of them would see whatever it was she saw in me.

I don't remember leaving the wedding, except for a brief glimpse of headlights panning through the yard as we pulled away from the house. I was resting my head on my arms and hands out the open passenger window of our SUV. I woke up unexpectedly to the powerful spray of cold water in my face. Jolting awake, I gasped, sucking water into my lungs, and choked out an undecipherable grunt. My head jerked up and my eyes struggled to come into focus as I heard the pressurized water against a hollow-sounding surface to my right.

In slow motion, my mind started piecing things together.

Okay, I'm in the car.
Why is my head out the window? Did I pass out like this?
And someone is spraying the car with water.
Someone... [choke]

I could hear the spray of water hitting the side of the car, growing louder and closer to me as I struggled to orient myself. Before I could move, I felt the cold water hitting me in the face, my arms flopping and flailing as I tried to shield my face and open my eyes.

The sound of the water stopped. [choke]

Mitch was standing before me, the garden hose in hand, having released the trigger and trapping the water behind the spout as the pressure built in the silence between us. "You threw up all over the side of the car," he said matter of factly, void of emotion. "I had to drive in the right lane the entire hour drive home so we wouldn't get pulled over. It was down the entire side of the car." He was upset but he was also taking care of business at the moment, so the anger stayed inside him.

My awareness panned out, taking in the scent of wine and bile in the summer night's air. Water splatters darkened the cuffs of Mitch's pants, and I watched him silently as he continued to rinse the evidence of my overindulgence from the exterior of our SUV. Gone was the whimsy of his tuxedo t-shirt under a velvet dinner jacket, replaced with the realization I had ruined the fun. Ashamed, I slowly unfolded my arms which ached from the trim of the window. The shape of it had molded trenches into my skin and I rubbed at their sensitive edges gently.

I rolled up my window, watching as more evidence of my excess smeared up with it. I gathered my things and got out of the car, closing the door behind me as I kept my eyes on the ground. I didn't remember throwing up out the side of the car, but I sobered a little knowing how much I had screwed up. I was trying so hard to fit in with a group I barely knew that I drank all night trying to hide my insecurities. I just kept thinking if I kept drinking, they would like me. *More alcohol means more fun, right?*

All night long, Mitch was there next to me, never leaving my side. He was there for me but, instead of bathing in that love and companionship, I pushed it aside to strive for their favor, too. I didn't take his cues to slow down or ask for a soda. I stopped giving a fuck that What's-His-Name's wife didn't like me. I slurred and spilled the wine as I refilled my glass until the storm passed and everyone started to leave.

Staring down at my feet as I followed Mitch to the back door of our building, I was devastated about what I had done. It was the first time I felt a part of my heart break because of how my drinking hurt someone I loved. We spoke little to each other as we cleaned ourselves up and settled into bed. "I love you," he said as he rolled my way for our nightly kiss.

"I love you," I said, my throat tight with a stifled sob.

I rolled over and turned off the light. As if it could protect me from how terrible I felt inside, I pulled the covers up tight to my neck and curled myself into a ball. I stared into the darkness of our merlot-colored bedroom and tried to fall asleep as my brain attempted to piece the shards of the night back together. I laid there mortified about what I had done. I had just wanted to enjoy the night out with Mitch, all dressed up on a romantic, summer evening. Instead, I wound up a loud, trashy, drunk mess at a lovely wedding full of people much classier than me.

Addiction is a slippery slope like that. In the beginning, drinking is fun and playful, buzzes feel like everything is covered in glitter. Shiny, illuminated, and reflecting light in every direction. But as repeated use begins altering the brain, the sparkle fades and the buzzes disappear. All that remains is the itch… *if I just have one more, I will feel that twinkle again.* The dopamine response changes. In the same way Pavlov conditioned dogs to salivate at the sound of the bell after routinely providing them treats as he rang it, our brain begins to 'salivate' at just the thought of alcohol acquisition. We begin to feel rewarded in not just the consumption of alcohol, but eventually in the pursuit of it (Schultz 2002).

As I grew up and tried to form connections and friendships, I didn't realize I was slowly conditioning myself to pursue alcohol, too. Even though underage kids don't drink as frequently as adults, studies have shown "more than 90 percent of all alcohol drinks consumed by youth are consumed through binge drinking" (NIAAA 2022). In my youth, it was no different. Long periods of not drinking were broken up by binge events on weekends, at slumber parties, and cabin getaways.

Invites to Jenny's cabin triggered excitement for swimming *and drinking*. Junior high locker room whispers of parties on the weekends sparked fireworks in my mind, and I could feel the kinetic energy grow beneath my skin. My friends and I would make plans for a rebellious adventure, and I quietly swallowed as my taste buds danced at the memory of tantalizing spirits. As I got older, however, it got more complicated.

As our roles as children morph into those more defined by expectations and the differentiation of girls and boys, my quest of belonging transformed, too. Eventually, being part of the crowd was less important than my role within it. Just like when I had my first drink, avoiding the social norm of flirting with the boys at Woodlake Lodge, I started to discover that I could use alcohol to define my role in the world.

Everything changed when I learned three lessons:
  – not all attention is good attention
  – monsters are real
  – you can drink to forget

Girls Who Wear Nail Polish

———

I knew what he was going to say before I asked but I had to try again anyway. I stopped and picked up a shiny glass bottle of ruby red nail polish with a splash of glitter as we passed the display and pleaded softly. "Dad, can I get this nail polish? I brought my allowance." Bringing my allowance was a rare occurrence that I had hoped would win me the nail polish. It was a vast improvement from the typical negotiations we had every Friday night at the grocery store. Dad kept walking as I begged him for an advance so I could get the latest *MAD* magazine that called to me from the shelf.

"No. You know what happens to girls who wear nail polish."

He said that for years any time I asked to buy nail polish or wear lip gloss. It was his answer to so many things. "You know what happens to girls with pierced ears." The statement always landed on my ears as a mystery as I had no idea what terrible outcome awaited such brazen girls. I just assumed he meant they ended up pregnant, the worst imaginable ending I could muster at the time.

Women like my mother and aunts, my grandmothers and their mothers before them, the suffragettes and civil rights activists all fought for decades to gain equality for women. They stormed a path for years and paved the way for my generation and beyond to roam safely and equally in this world. We were told we could do anything we set our hopeful hearts on. We were liberated and free to be whoever we wanted to be. Or so I believed.

By high school, I cast off his cloudy reasoning as a joke. "Sure, Dad. And my car will turn into a pumpkin if I'm not home by curfew," I would reply with a heavy layer of snark, testing the waters on what I could get away with while still being an obedient child.

Standing by the colorful display, I mustered up a tiny mound of defiance and pushed back. "Why?" I demanded with my feet grounded firmly in place. He didn't turn around or miss a step, he just kept walking without saying a word. He never did tell me what *it* was. He left me to fill in the blanks with my own imagination, unable to truly comprehend what horrors lie out in the world.

In reality, pain and suffering are inevitable parts of life. No matter how much parents care for and protect their children, hurt will always find a way in. How could they save me from everything when being a girl in this society wasn't always a safe thing to be?

* * *

The sleepy town I grew up in was a sheltered one where nothing scandalous happened outside of the occasional high school pranks and keg parties. As kids, we explored every inch of the town on bicycles, then graduated to cars once any one of our friends got their driver's license. It was a predictable and simple place to grow up, yet Dad always tried to prepare me for the worst.

We slept with the doors locked and windows closed except for the second floor. He taught me to scan my surroundings in parking lots every time I left a store, darting my eyes around looking for possible danger. Watching for mysterious feet hiding on the far side of our car. "There's bad people out there who could hurt you, kiddo. You can never be too prepared." It had only been six years since the nationally known disappearance of Jacob Wetterling, a young Minnesota boy kidnapped from an even smaller town than ours.

I didn't believe bad things happened in our secure little town until the day our morning bus driver skipped the last pick-up, driving straight past a classmate's home surrounded in yellow ribbons. "Is that police tape?" rose in whispers from each row of seats as we continued to school.

Our high school principal addressed us on the morning video announcements, his voice soft and somber, validating the expanse of fear that rolled within me. Slowly and meticulously, he picked the best words anyone could use to tell an entire student body that one of our classmates was murdered overnight. We came to find out later the girl's boyfriend killed her and her mother with a shotgun in the middle of the night. She was trying to break up with him and he snapped, later found with a kill list in his pocket once the authorities arrested him.

Everything our community understood about safety and the innocence of youth crumbled. Our relaxed, peaceful little town quickly snapped into a bitter, stunned, and cautious place. Unexpectedly, Dad's words came back to me. "You know what happens to girls who..." I started to see the ominous truth form before me. My naive world was a lot bigger than I ever knew and a lot scarier than I ever imagined.

* * *

In the summer before my senior year of high school, I rejoined a pair of my friends on a two-week job at the state fair. It was our second year working for the same family-owned dessert stand. Even though we pulled thirteen-hour days for the twelve-day stretch, it felt to me like summer camp. We'd all stay at Stella's huge fancy house for two weeks, carpooling together, sweating off pounds in the August heat, and banking a lot of dough in the process. After long days of work, we'd stop off at a nearby lake on our way home. We would strip down to our sports bras and underwear and run full speed into the dark, still water, our laughter ricocheting off the shoreline trees. The sounds disappeared into the night sky with all the stressors of the day while the lake rinsed away the stench.

With only a few days left to work, our manager started acting differently around me, but only when I was alone. Maybe it was because I was the more timid one, obedient and submissive. In the lulls between customers, he would walk up and stand next to me, never saying a word. He just stood there. Close. So close. I never knew what to do. If he wasn't ignoring me, he was barking orders at me to do extra work. "Pick that up! Put this away! Take that box to the other food stand."

He was a short, round, foul-smelling man with a permanent scowl on his face. He had started to poke at me with insults about my crooked front tooth, the plainness of my makeup-less face, his distaste of my tomboy style. I liked the owners of the dessert stand and loved the time with my friends both summers we worked for them. That disgusting excuse for a human was an annoyance we had to tolerate to get through each shift. The three of us all hated him for being a jerk and something in that shared disgust made it all that more bearable.

He shoved a bucket of hot soapy water across the metal counter toward me on the last night as us girls were getting excited to close up shop for the season. "Make sure you get the bottom of the refrigerator. It's disgusting!" he snarled before storming off. I grabbed the bucket and knelt on the concrete floor, sighing to myself as I opened the fridge to begin cleaning. I was still scrubbing the inside when he returned minutes later, standing too close for my comfort yet again.

He cleared his throat to get my attention, but not loud enough for the other girls to hear. They were only ten feet away serving customers as he inched closer. "While you're down there…" he said suggestively as the words trailed off into the sounds of people ambling about the food building. He laughed at his own words, proud of his own obscenity. I was only seventeen, but I knew what he meant. I knew because every boy in school said it to any girl found kneeling in public. As if hearing "while you're down there" was all a gal needed to agree. "Hey, yeah, good idea! How about I give you a blow job?" No, that's not how it works.

But this was different. I could laugh at the boys at school and shove them off their chair in disgust. I was certain they would never hurt me. When it came to this manager, however, my intuition knew no innocent intentions could be hidden in actions like his.

His shadow loomed over me like an eclipse as I knelt on the wet concrete. My bare knees shifted beneath me as the imbalance of power held me in place. Frozen like a rabbit in the eyes of its predator, motionless, my eyes focused on my hands as they began to tremble. *Maybe if I just freeze, if I play dead, he will lose interest and move on. Please... please. Just go away!*

I held my position without moving, waiting for someone, anyone, to help me. No one came. He stood there for a few agonizing moments as I held my breath and desperately tried to stifle a cry. Without another word, he eventually turned and left. I watched a single tear fall from my cheek, eyes still glued to my hand, clenching the sponge as if it could somehow right my upturned world. Once I gathered myself, I hurriedly finished cleaning the kitchen cooler and rushed through the rest of our closing duties without speaking. I kept my eyes on the ground until we walked out to Stella's car that night, too afraid of seeing the real monster again.

I didn't say anything to the girls after we left but the fear stuck to me like the perspiration on my skin. I sat in the back seat and rubbed at my arms, hands gliding over the slickness leftover from the grease and sweat. They laughed and recounted silly, light-hearted experiences we'd had that summer at the fair. I huffed and smiled softly at each one.

Somewhere deep down inside, the damage was already done.

Summer ended and senior year started, a whirl of classes, homework, joining clubs, and making homecoming plans. I came home from school one Friday afternoon to an empty house. Dad had left for a weekend hunting trip, and I was finally allowed to stay home alone for the first time. I noticed the blinking light on our kitchen answering machine as I set my keys on the counter. *Dad's worried already,* I joked to myself as I walked over to press play.

Rather than hearing my dad, I was startled immediately by a familiar gravelly voice. The sound of my former manager's voice was metered and haunting, the way a movie villain taunts and intimidates a cornered victim. As he reminisced about "our time together" on the tape, I pictured him alone in a dark room, eyes glossy and mouth formed in a snarl. "My old high school is the opponent for your homecoming football game. Watch for me. I'll come find you during the game."

The air escaped my lungs, and I clasped a hand over my mouth. I stopped the tape and ran to check that I had locked the door when I'd come in. I checked the garage door and made sure the patio door was locked too. I ran from window to window and closed the shades. Breathless, I returned to the kitchen and stared at the phone on the wall.

If it were any other game, I could have just skipped it. But this was homecoming, and I was the student mascot. I was scheduled to don my huge, stuffy cougar suit and perform in a solo half-time routine. There would be nowhere to hide.

Suddenly, I felt so vulnerable. So exposed. *How did he get my number? Does he know where I live? Did he know I was going to be home alone?* I was too afraid to be by myself and definitely too terrified to stay home. I called up some friends who I knew would be free and found a party to surround me with people and a safe place to crash for the night.

I threw some clothes in a duffle bag, fed the cat, and turned on every light in the house. I locked it up and left a message on my dad's cell phone, trying to sound as calm and normal as I could, "Dad, I'm staying at Stella's while you're away. I love you."

We spent the evening with a few dozen friends huddled close to a bonfire like we did most weekends. One guy in our grade looked at least twenty-five and could buy beer without issue. His parents had a three-acre wooded plot on the edge of town and let us do whatever we wanted. His yard became a regular oasis, a hidden retreat within the trees. I confided with Stella about the voicemail as we sauntered off in the dark to pee behind some tall oaks at the border of the fire's glow. "What a fucking creep!" she shouted loud enough to turn a few heads our way.

"Shhh. This is really freaking me out. I never told you what he said that last night of work," I dropped the volume of my voice and stood closer to her before we returned to the fire. She was appalled but, like me, had no idea what to do.

"He's a creep! Let's go back, have another beer, and forget him. C'mon, it'll be fine. Let's go have some fun," her reassurance was genuine.

I stuck to my friends and the light of the fire, the safety of them both making it a little easier to breathe. Another beer rolled down my throat as I watched the boys performing goofy stunts to impress the girls. The giggles and jokes from the group warming by the blaze felt like home. I sat quietly, just happy to be safe in that moment. Then, unexpectedly, I heard the voice on the answering machine again as if it had followed me there. I chugged the rest of my beer and headed to a table of colorful shot glasses lying in sticky pools of cinnamon and apple-flavored booze.

"Who wants to do shots with me?" I cajoled my classmates with a crooked grin, knowing this plan was all about me disguised as a way to entertain them.

As the night went on, each drink made the danger seem smaller, quieter, farther away. I drank until I left my dinner behind a tree in the yard and my only focus was my inability to walk a straight line. I woke with a terrible hangover the next morning and stared at the ceiling as if I had opened my eyes to a new world. I had felt safe in the company of my friends that night and found a way to quell the terrifying thoughts inside my head.

The next month escalated into failed assignments and sleepless nights; two things painfully new to me. I lost my ability to maintain focus in class or recall everything I had studied as I stared down at each test. I got pulled out of AP chem the week of homecoming and sent to the counselor's office. I sat down on a worn-out chair in his dimly lit room and twisted my fingers together in my lap waiting for him to tell me why we were there. He spoke softly and began expressing concern in the change of my behavior and test scores. "You're a straight-A student, Kristy. Do you want to talk about what's going on?" Mr. Smith asked gently, hands resting on the bare wooden desk between us.

I took a breath, looked down at my intertwined digits, and let it all out. Homecoming was less than a week away and I was the school mascot. "I can't just *not go* to homecoming, but he called my house! He said he's going to be there, and I don't know what to do." He listened courageously as I poured out my dread, the feeling of being watched, how I couldn't sleep. I rambled and stumbled over my words, stopping to listen only when he looked me in the eyes and promised to help. "I'm scared," I finished, wiping at the tears as they pushed through the corners of my eyes. The school called both my parents and my mom was waiting at our house by the time I got off school.

"What did you do?" Dad asked me with a furrow in his brow. Behind his rough bravado was a tender, loving heart deep inside that tried to protect me at all costs. But, in the moment, I felt accused of something I didn't do.

"Nothing!" I cried out in honest desperation. Sadly, my dad had the same response most of society had at that time in the nineties and sometimes still does. How women and girls dressed, how they acted, or where they went were blame enough to justify any man's harm of them. Hell, it wasn't until 1993 that it was finally made illegal to rape your spouse in all fifty US states (2004). How could we not still expect to be treated like objects? Belongings? Like caged animals, we're allowed to live safely if we obey the rules and expectations. But step out of the cage and you're on your own.

The bright lights in the living room made it feel like an interrogation until my mom spoke up in a way I had never seen before. Her voice was bold and harsh, her energy morphing into something almost palpable before my eyes. My mom only stood five-foot-four, but that night she looked like she was 6 feet tall, staring Dad directly in the eyes with a fury that both frightened and soothed me. She defended me ferociously, the way every woman and girl who has been questioned about their own behavior when violated by men should be defended.

"He's a grown man who should **never** treat a woman, a CHILD, this way. She's a child! Nothing she did made him do this. He is a sick man!" There, with her silky, smooth hand holding mine firmly, yet never too tight, it felt as though Mom poured her fire into me. She never moved from my side as she held the line she drew in the living room that night.

I cried softly as they fought yet felt relieved to no longer be going through it alone. I don't know if one of them surrendered or said the magic word but suddenly, late into the night, the jagged edge that remained between them dissolved. They finally came to realize the most important part: we were all on the same side. The enemy was miles away and we were only going to be stronger if we stuck together.

The tension fizzled to a steady hum and the relief brought a heavy fatigue with it. I felt my puffy eyes swell and heave with the weight of exhaustion and excused myself for bed. I hugged Dad then walked over to Mom with a quiver in my chin. I squeezed her hand and hugged her goodbye knowing she'd be gone by the time I woke up. I ran up the yellow carpeted stairs to my room and laid down in my bed, clutching my favorite purple stuffed dinosaur from childhood. I looked down at my hands by the faint nightlight in the hall. My plain, unpainted nails were gnawed down so short they were just shy of bleeding and my fingers throbbed as I took them in.

I thought bad things only happen to girls who wore nail polish. I didn't do anything wrong. Why can't this all go away?

By the end of the week, my parents had teamed up to request a restraining order, and the school promised me a personal police escort to stay with me throughout the homecoming game. I never saw him again, but the trepidation never left me. Constantly checking the backseat of my car, searching the stands at games, watching for movement in the dark.

I spent the rest of the year trying to be invisible yet never alone. I started wearing oversized Metallica t-shirts and baggie jeans in an attempt to thwart any male interest that might look my way. At parties, I became the jester, an entertainer. I would drink heavily and channel my favorite comedians, impersonating quirky characters and reciting movie lines: Gilda Radner when she was on *Saturday Night Live*, Jim Carrey of the *In Living Color* days, John Candy as Uncle Buck.

I would do shots and try to make my friends laugh with terrible accents. I got up on tables and sang at the top of my lungs. I carried a Zippo lighter just to look edgy and cool, playing a character of someone less anxious than myself. I became someone who helped chug the bottle before we spun it and, when we played "Truth or Dare," I always picked dare. Anything that kept the alcohol coming and the distractions in constant supply. Booze flooded the cavernous room in my mind where the worries ran free, drowning out their cries as each mouthful filled the space. Glass after glass, the frantic and foreboding voices would choke and try to scream until they bobbed silently in the ocean of booze that filled me.

I used to believe if I could make and follow my own rules it meant I was disciplined. Responsible. I did my homework as soon as I got home from school each day. That meant I was a good student. I practiced my slap shot on and off the ice. That made me a dedicated hockey player. I only drank on the weekends with friends. That meant I didn't have a problem with alcohol. If I don't drink and drive, I'm a responsible drinker. The more control I had over things meant I could keep my world safe and calm.

Gabor Maté was a presenter at TEDx Rio in 2012 where he spoke about the immense power addiction has over its sufferers. He explained addiction as "any behavior that gives you temporary relief, temporary pleasure, but in the long term causes harm, has some negative consequences, and you can't give it up despite those negative consequences" (Maté 2012). I never thought I was addicted to alcohol until that night at the QotSA concert. Or at least that was the first time I admitted it. Looking back now, I can see my attachments. My reliance and dependence on alcohol as an escape was multifaceted and decades old.

As I wrapped up high school and prepared to venture off into the world, I did so with a false sense of reality. I thought I was safe behind the rules I had made for myself and the persona I had created. I was truly using alcohol as a shield between myself and the life I was trying to exist in. Eventually, I would create so many rules of how I needed to act to stay safe that I would completely lose touch with who I was.

* * *

And what about those girls who wear nail polish?

I pushed back on my dad before every dance and weekend at Jenny's cabin to beg permission to wear nail polish until he finally caved and said, "Fine, but only your toes." Maybe he was giving this kid who was having a hard time a break. Maybe he knew I was growing up and not responding was no longer an acceptable reply. Either way, I would slowly and methodically paint my toenails one at a time in bright reds and pinks. I moved purposely from one tiny toenail to the next as I sang along to whatever spun on the record player in my room.

Once I moved away to college, I started painting my nails to stop myself from chewing them. It was how I justified my sparkly fingertips when I returned home for holidays, feeling so grown up in my sensibility. I have always loved the process of painting my nails. Dabbing the brush into the smooth bottle then raising it up to watch a shiny colored drop fall in slow motion. The concentration clears my mind and for a few minutes, my worries head out for a smoke break. I take my time to do absolutely nothing for a few minutes so they can dry, all the while admiring my little artistic flare. The smallest dose of rebellion and self-care each week that I seldom reschedule.

Now, you'll rarely see me without nail polish or, at minimum, fragments of paint remaining after a long day of gardening with my hands in the warm soil. I always finish my thumbs and middle fingers with a layer of sparkles. The thumb to add emphasis when I wink and say, "Good job."

The middle ones… those are for driving home an important point:

Do not fuck with girls who wear nail polish.

Camouflage

———

"What do you think the party will be like?" I asked Robin from across her dorm room as I applied mascara lightly to my upper lashes. She pulled a curved mascara wand over her long lashes and looked at me through the mirror. "I bet they're just like the high school ones. Just… better." She smiled reassuringly and I believed her.

"I hope the guys are hotter!" I said, winking back at her. In all honesty, I only hoped to have a little fun.

We both laughed and returned to primping as *Led Zeppelin IV* spun on the turntable. Robin and I had been friends since high school and got closer when we moved into dorm rooms just two floors from each other. She was one of a small handful of friends that also ventured north to Duluth for our studies, and they became my closest friends in the dorms. A familiar piece of home to stay close to.

College parties will be just like back home. I got this. Famous last words to rely on before heading out for our first house party. In high school, I had found my place in the crowd by being brave enough to drink anything and dumb enough to never say "stop" when it came time to refilling my drink. I'd stumble off at some point each night and empty my stomach full of booze behind a tree in the back yard, then teeter back with arms raised victoriously overhead. "Puke 'n rally!" I shouted as I bobbled, calling for the crowd's reprise as I refilled my plastic cup. But, in college, I was suddenly back to being nobody and had to find a way to survive all over again.

Robin and I met up with a few more friends on the first floor of our building and followed one of the girls who wrote the address to the party on her hand. Rather than a backyard gathering with friends we knew, we stepped into a house jammed with underaged coeds, sticky floors, and furniture made out of empty cardboard beer boxes. Five dollars got you a plastic cup to carry down sketchy basement stairs in search of the rumored kegs as other booze-guzzling boys and girls tried to weave back up the narrow passage and rejoin the party. We stuck to one another like glue as we shyly filled our glasses in the unfinished basement and made our own ascent back to the loud music above.

As the night grew on and the liquor started to melt my nervousness, I rallied my friends to join in the shots and keg stands. When my turn came, I gripped the wet, cold metal handles on top, taking a deep breath as I listened to the ice jostling in the plastic bin it rested in. I tucked my t-shirt into the front of my pants and gave them a nod. I felt weightless when the biggest guys at the party hoisted my feet up in the air, inches from the ceiling. The crowd chanted, "Chug, chug!" as one of the guys holding my feet began to count.

"One, two, three," his voice deep and husky as I tried to focus on drinking the cold beer as quickly as it poured into my mouth from the hose.

Swallow. Quick breath through your nose. Hold it. Chug. Swallow.

"Six, seven, eight." I kept drinking until I choked, and beer exploded out my nose. The guys put me down gently and the small group of coeds in the basement cheered as I wiped my face clear with the back of my hand.

Beer was spilled all around us, dampening the old wooden floors and mismatched furniture in all the rooms. By the time we stumbled back to our dorm that night, my mind was swimming with keg beer and slivers of memories of things I wasn't sure I had really seen. Shouts of girls gone wild sent barely legal drunk guys trampling down the halls for a chance to spy some titties. Over-served gals puking in pitchers. Handfuls of guys cramming into the bathroom to simultaneously piss in the tub to *save water!* Ew.

I crawled up into my lofted bed and smiled to myself as I switched off the reading light. *I got this.*

* * *

In nature and warfare, camouflage is used as a form of protection from predators or enemy troops. Some types of camo allow an organism to blend in with their surroundings, like a lizard changing its color to match the rock it crouches on as a predator looks past. Some creatures, like the mimic octopus, are capable of morphing the shape of its body to resemble a sea snake, crab, or jellyfish. It's fascinating the way it undulates through water, pretending to be something completely different than itself to keep safe from harm.

Not unlike humans at all.

In high school, I camouflaged my need for companionship by participating in most of the extracurriculars our school had to offer. Spanish club, yearbook, National Honor Society, the weightlifting and hockey teams, drama and speech. Every last one of them. While they looked impressive on a college application and earned me the title *Most School Spirit* senior year, they really just kept me from feeling alone.

While college was only two hours from home, it felt like I was a world away from everything I knew. Luckily, I had a solid group of friends that always reminded me of the place I longed for, no matter how independent I was trying to be. Robin was like a wise sister and the six guys like my goofy brothers. I didn't feel like I had to hide when I was with them.

I struggled to make friends in the lecture halls crammed with four hundred other young adults, so I stuck to my small group of my high school friends and our new roommates whenever I needed company. A month into classes, a few of us went to an open house for all the campus clubs, filled with tables of students from every sports team and group you could imagine. I signed up for a work study program and joined the intramural rugby team with Robin and one of the guys we knew as a way for us to meet people. Rugby seemed like a great way to blow off steam and a natural sport to try after years of taking and doling out hits playing hockey in high school. I picked it up quickly and was proud when I was added to the starting lineup as a freshman.

In rugby, the battle on the field was intense. Learning to hit someone hard enough to knock them off their feet without pads required me to channel all my aggression unapologetically. When I played hockey, the hits didn't hurt nearly as much, and there was always an ice pack waiting for me at home. Rugby demanded an entirely new level of toughness I was excited to learn.

Once each game ended, win, lose, or draw, the party began. Both teams would venture off to the hosting "rugby house" still sweaty and bloody from the match that preceded. The house reminded me of my favorite college movie, *Animal House*, with soggy floors in the living room and empty kegs and discarded cups strewn across the concrete floor of the basement.

I shouldn't have been surprised when showing up to the party as a rookie required two shots of Wild Turkey and a slammed beer as cost of entry. Still dehydrated and hungry, worn down from the match, we did as we were told. With brains spinning and stomachs sloshing with liquids, we would be released to enjoy the party and mingle with the rest of the players. As the evening waned, the kegs would get changed out to something better than Milwaukee's Best as the captains and their cohorts hunted us down with Sharpies in hand. We sat willingly, laughing side by side as they wrote all over our faces. To me it was just the price of admission. So was drinking. *You must be THIS WASTED to ride this ride.*

I delighted on the inside with a homesick sense of belonging. I was becoming one of them.

We entered a tournament in St. Paul, MN, that required us to drive down to the city for a single day of back to back matches and a couple nights' stay in town. It was so close to mine and Robin's hometown that we chose to return to our family homes for free lodging, laundry, and the comfort of our own beds. It was nice to be home and see my dad before I left for the matches the first morning, a vast departure from the breakfast that would come the following day.

After our duels of the day, we headed to a private after-hours party at a brewery close to the polo grounds we played on. I remember the hesitation in my chest as we walked up to the brewery doors that evening. I was eighteen years old and had never tried ordering a drink in a bar aside from that first margarita. The drinking age in Minnesota is twenty-one years old but our captains swore that we'd be fine as long as we pretended we were of age. I breathed a sigh of relief as I was granted entry simply on my word.

"You're twenty-one, right?"

I added three years to my birth year and nodded shyly as I gave my practiced lie. "Yep. Born June 1978. Sorry, I forgot my ID," I feigned as I patted the empty pockets of my rugby shorts. No ID. No money. No cellphone. The team had reserved the place for our own private party. All we had to do was show up and they took care of the rest.

Like most rugby parties, the night was a blur. It felt as though I moved through a secret existence, feet navigating a sticky bar floor with drink in hand, barely old enough to fend for myself in the real world. The beer was flowing from taps and pitchers everywhere I turned. I hid my eyes from making contact with others when I felt my balance give out and tried to avoid the commands to chug more beer.

Maybe it was because they knew we were underaged and would do anything to be at a private party in a brewery, but something lurked in the dark alcoves of the bar that night. Something in the air encouraged the captains to narrow in on our personal limits, unrelenting with pitchers of beers and permanent markers. Hellbent on breaking us down.

As myself and the other rookies mingled about the bar, we were often plopped down onto the black leather barstools as Sharpies were passed around. We were given pints to guzzle as they turned every inch of our faces into a bathroom wall with crass drawings and sayings to make an average person flinch: crude drawings of tits and penises, nicknames, and body-shaming one-liners. Girls were tagged with labels like "dirty whore" and "power slut" across their foreheads. Guys were branded "limp dick" and "blue balls." The rookies traded sympathetic glances, consoling each other through our shared debasing.

Why we kept coming to these parties after being treated that way was a mystery then, but now it's a sad reflection to look back on. To me, loneliness was a palpable ache I could touch in the center of my chest. It restricted my breathing and tensed my muscles outside of my control. Researchers have found the fear of social rejection activates the same sections of the brain that are activated during physical pain. Even the "mere visual appearance of exclusion" was enough to stimulate the same neurological response as physical injury (Eisenberger, Lieberman, Williams 2003). I guess somewhere in that ache of loneliness I found relief in just being with these people, whether I was truly accepted or not.

I remember getting dropped off at home in the middle of the night. I walked up the concrete path and stairs on unsteady legs, hands open and arms outstretched in my beer-soaked jersey, and a foul taste in my mouth. I fumbled the key into the lock and tried to stay silent as I navigated the darkness inside. I peed one last time then slowly tiptoed up the carpeted stairs that climbed to my room.

Plush carpet beneath my feet was welcoming and comforting as I tried to dodge the creaky stairs I had learned over the years. I held my breath in fear of waking my dad in the silence of the night. Gingerly, I crawled into bed and immediately passed out. By the time morning came, I was still in the exact same position, stiff from the rigidity of it.

I walked slowly down the stairs and straight to the kitchen, sitting down at the wooden kitchen table of my childhood home with a bowl of sugary cereal. We rarely ever ate at the table, but Dad joined me in the kitchen that morning. He sat across from me but didn't say a word. I tried to regal my dad with stories of our matches, ending most sentences with a rising inflection as if I kept asking if he was proud yet. He seemed disinterested and avoided most attempts at eye contact. My hangover was all-consuming, and I leaned so heavily into my pride-seeking that I didn't see the red flags in front of me.

Once I finished my cereal, I washed my dishes and put them away. I walked into the bathroom to brush my teeth before getting ready to return to the dorms. I closed the door behind me and looked in the mirror. That's when I saw it.

My eyes were bloodshot and weighed down with plump bags that hung low beneath them, my skin pale beneath permanent marker tattoos all over my face. I blinked and looked up at the reflection of my forehead in the mirror, ready to roll my eyes at whatever stupid thing they wrote this time.

"CUM DUMPSTER."

"CUM DUMPSTER," in thick, black letters across my forehead. With my eyes, I followed the large outline of an arrow that began just below the words. I trailed the lines down my cheek until they took a sharp turn to point directly at the side of my mouth. Mortified, I stood unmoving before the mirror as the steaming water ran from the faucet. *"Cum dumpster,"* I choked out in a whisper to myself, an appalled whimper lodged in my throat.

I grabbed a wash rag, pumped the soap dispenser repeatedly, and proceeded to scrub my face in a panic. They had written "slut," "bitch," and "cunt" on me repeatedly but never once had it hurt me like this. I was still a virgin, still so timid around the opposite sex. It felt like an accusation, and I was ashamed down to the core of my soul. *But I've never...* The thought faded into a whimper as I got back to work. The ink had soaked deep into my pores and refused to disappear, so I added more soap to the stained cloth and scrubbed harder.

I walked around all night with this label on my face. I talked to my captains. I talked to that hot guy on the other team. To the bartenders. Oh my god, what did they think of me? Did he really think I'm like that? Who else did I see? Dad. Oh fuck, Dad saw this and read this, and oh shit he must think I'm horrible. But I don't. I'm not.

I emerged from the bathroom with my face as raw as my emotions, crimson from the vigorous scrubbing and humiliation. I snuck back up to my room to pack for my return away from my dad's judging eyes. Once packed, I sat on the end of my bed until Robin pulled up in our driveway to collect me. He never spoke about the way he had found me that morning and neither did I. I held my breath and gave him a hesitant hug goodbye, hoping he somehow still approved of me.

I walked down our steps and climbed into her car, watching the house in silence as she backed out of my driveway. As we pulled out of town, both of us hungover from the night before, I told her about what had happened with Dad and how rattled I felt. She burst out laughing just as I expected she would, and I found a moment to laugh with her at my own expense. Emotionally wounded, I gazed out the side window in silence.

I could still feel the outline of each letter I had frantically scoured from my pink flesh. The captains crossed a line that night, and I couldn't see a way to move forward past it. *How much am I willing to compromise myself to be part of this team?*

There is a moth found in tropical rainforests of Asia known as the Atlas moth, or *Attacus atlas*. Their wingspan can stretch up to nine inches, making it one of the largest moths in the world. More impressive than the size of the massive wings are the remarkable patterns found on their delicate canvases. The tips of the wings are formed into the shapes of cobra heads, rounded, complete with eyes and scale markings that resemble the dangerous snakes. To keep birds and lizards from attacking it, the Atlas moth moves its wings with a fluid sway resembling the hypnotic undulations of a cobra's neck.

Sure, I was desperate to fit in. But not **that** desperate.

* * *

Back at the dorms, I pushed the memory of the rugby tournament deep down inside with the same avoidant edge used to shove my duffle bag into its corner of my closet. I was still charged with anger and my body buzzed with anxious energy. I sat quickly at my desk to send a clipped email to our rugby captains, quitting the team without apology or explanation. "How will I ever look my dad in the eyes again, you bitches!" I snapped at the monitor as I clicked send.

I didn't know how to put words to the distress inside me with Robin or the other girls and we eventually drifted apart. I couldn't understand why I was so shaken but the other girls weren't. I took it to mean that I wasn't as grown up as them. Not as sophisticated. Too soft, not as tough. I carried around a massive sense of failure around for days, softly crying myself to sleep.

I eventually found comfort back with the boys from home, smoking weed and playing video games to pass the time away. I had known some of these guys since we roamed the yard in diapers, making comfort in vast supply and all pressure was out the door. With them, it was like home. I could go back to being 'just one of the guys.' It was a safe space to hover in where I had the friendship and protection of six trustworthy friends, but no sexual obligation to any of them. Close to the inner circle, yet too close to be seen as an interest.

When we went to parties, I simply wanted to drink with my friends and have a good time. And if you're a late-blooming virgin who wants to be left alone, what better way than showing up with six dudes? Each of them was willing to step in as my boyfriend if I was being harassed by drunk morons. I exchanged their chivalry by graciously talking them up to the ladies that sparked their interest, always putting in a good word. Weekends were raucous as we hiked through town at night to each party, knocking back beers, laughing at wet belches, then stumbling uphill back to our dorms before dawn.

Alcohol becomes an addiction by generating associations within your brain. The more I leaned into my role as one of the guys, the safer I felt. I convinced myself I was in control of the way I was drinking. Creating that clown persona, the entertaining boozehound slamming drinks, was proof I knew what I was doing. *Right.* The hidden truth was alcohol was the reason I ever invented the clown at all. A mask.

My disguise that allowed me to justify the large quantities I would drink. An excuse to binge until I couldn't hear my thoughts any longer. A cover to drown my feelings in a way everyone could accept.

I pretended to be who I needed to in order to get drunk. I kept getting wasted over and over to escape being alone in my head. Alone with myself.

Who, Me?

———

Not all memories are created equal. And with blackouts, it turns out, they were never actually created at all.

I used to believe if you completely forgot what happened during a heavy bout of drinking it was because alcohol killed those brain cells. No. Well, yes, alcohol does kill brain cells but that's not what causes blackouts. Studies have found that rapid or high-volume consumption of alcohol that leads to blackouts is due to alcohol's effect on the hippocampus, the region of the brain responsible for memory formation. The drinker is fully awake but, as the blood alcohol level in the body increases, it prevents the brain from transferring memories from short-term to long-term storage (NIAAA 2021).

I remember when I was in my early twenties drinking screwdrivers at brunch with my girlfriends, a little hair of the dog to chase away our hangovers as we laughed about what happened the night before. We all snickered as they told me stories of things I couldn't recall. Back then it seemed like innocent fun, not a sign of a bigger problem. Not at all the precursor of bad things to come.

It wasn't until I finally got sober for good and started working through the pain of all my blacked-out mishaps that old memories of Emma returned to me.

* * *

Back when I worked at the state fair with Stella, another friend and I would sleep at Stella's house for the two-week stint. The three of us girls would have the entire finished basement to ourselves which ensured we wouldn't disturb anyone with our early mornings and by coming home late each night. She lived on the nice end of town with her parents and two older sisters in the biggest house I'd ever seen. With gorgeous, tiled floors, floor-to-ceiling windows, and a vacuum system that ran through the walls, everything looked and felt priceless.

Living at Stella's house felt like I was living out *The Baby-sitters Club* books I binged as a child. We would come home each night with greasy faces, soaked in our own sweat and smelling of fried food. Stella's mom, Emma, would come down to the basement with bowls of ice cream to ask about our adventures as we cleaned ourselves up for bed. We would sit perched on leather high-top chairs along their modern basement bar laughing with ice cream-smeared grins, recounting the outrageous things we had seen each day.

Emma would spend the late hours with us until we tired, moving off to our spare beds to sleep before repeating the routine again the next day: Rise before the sun, find the closest parking we could, scramble to the dessert booth, schlep treats for thirteen hours, return home, giggle and share, sleep, repeat.

One night as we sat at the bar in Stella's basement, I scooped large spoonfuls of cookie dough ice cream into my mouth as I watched Emma. She floated around behind the bar with an iced beverage in hand, telling jokes and stories to the three of us weary girls with a small and a subtle dance to her step. She would raise her arms out to her sides almost as if she was conducting a hidden orchestra playing a soundtrack to amplify her fables. The amber liquid in the glass sloshed up over the edges when she got excited, and I knew by her rosy cheeks it was likely her favorite bourbon.

Stella leaned over and whispered, "She's sleepwalking."

I stopped trying to mash the mound of ice cream around in my mouth, afraid to move as I tried to replay what she said in my head. *Did I hear that correctly?* Stella leaned in closer as she continued. "She doesn't even know what she's doing. She won't remember this in the morning," she nodded toward her mother and returned to her own bowl of frozen relief after the long summer day's heat.

I stared at Emma as if I was on a movie set watching an actress perform a scene, no longer listening to a word she was saying as I focused on her every move. "People drink when they sleepwalk?" I whispered back in bewilderment as I watched her. I tuned back into her stories and started to engage with questions, turning myself into a research student trying to observe the never-before seen apparition in front of me.

In reality, it's almost impossible to tell if someone is blackout drunk just by looking at them. Researchers have found that people in a blackout state from alcohol can walk, dance, hold conversations, drive a car, or even have sex. In a publication by the National Institute on Alcohol Abuse and Alcoholism, they state "blackouts often occur at blood-alcohol (BAC) levels of 0.16 or higher (double the legal limit in most states to drive)." People in a blackout state are still awake but their brain does not form new memories during that time (NIAAA 2021).

At levels of intoxication like this, alcohol impairs nearly all cognitive abilities. Aside from blocking memory formation, the brain's ability to hold attention, make decisions, control impulses, or use good judgment also become significantly impaired.

Sure enough, the next day, Emma wouldn't remember a thing. But she never let on that our stories were unfamiliar, smiling and nodding and giggling along with us the next night as if nothing was amiss. Later in life, I tried to insert that same fake response into my own life. Nodding in agreement when my husband brought up events from the night before that sounded like someone else's life. Reminiscing with my friends over concerts attended, I let them lead the storytelling. Listening intently while I worked to assemble some picture in my mind where the only thing there was a completely black and bottomless void.

After we graduated, Stella's parents got a divorce and Emma found a place of her own. Emma would tell me she was happy and enjoying life when we'd run into each other. Then, a few years later, she was found dead of a brain aneurysm. Alone on the kitchen floor, with an empty glass on the counter, they say she died quickly. Whispers of her heavy drinking stained conversations at her wake and funeral. *Do you think her drinking was the cause?* My heart broke with her passing and felt trampled by the way some people spoke about her after she was gone.

After the funeral, a group of us gathered at a friend's home to comfort one another over mixed drinks and beers. We tried to make sense of the tragedy. Tried to understand how life goes on for anyone after the loss of a parent. I excused myself to the bathroom, taking a moment to be alone and let my guard down a moment to cry. Heartbroken tears streamed down my face in the silent space as the irony of the moment sank in. Here we were relying on alcohol for comfort even though we were mourning the loss of someone we believed succumbed to its ill effects. *Yeah, but it won't happen to **me**.*

When memories of that night with Emma and my friends came back to me, I saw it through a new lens. What if Emma had actually been blackout drunk instead of sleepwalking? Had she told the girls it was just sleepwalking to lessen the seriousness of what they witnessed? Emma had a huge, selfless heart that worked tirelessly to ensure everyone was taken care of. I would understand if she had chosen to make a hard reality easier for her daughters to experience.

In the fifteen or more years following her death until I finally got sober, I would often envision those same whispers at my own funeral someday. *Is this how I'll be remembered, too?*

* * *

Coming out of a blackout while the party is still going is tricky.

Rather than waking up in my own bed the morning after a night of drinking, there were a few times I came back to reality somewhere I hadn't left off. A few movies and TV shows of my childhood mirrored this moment. In *Back to the Future*, Marty McFly time-travels to his parent's high school years and creates a false reality as the new kid in school. In the TV show *Quantum Leap*, Dr. Beckett would time travel only to awake in another person's body with a mission to right some historical wrong. Every week, he lived a period of time in someone else's life, faking his way through his first few moments in his new world as he took in the scene around him. Once he had his bearings, he lived their life until he would rewrite history and earn a new "leap" that could possibly return him to his actual life and time.

The first time it happened, I found myself intimately entangled with the guy at the bar I'd been flirting with for a couple weeks. My eyes came into focus mid-kiss, and I hustled to figure out whose face was pressed against mine. Every one of my senses fired in urgency, taking in my surroundings. The dark room, the smell of his deodorant, soft music playing somewhere nearby. All the while my arms held on to him prepared to flee yet my lips kept doing what was expected of them.

As the pieces fell into place and I realized where I was, I discarded my apprehension like a warning label and tried to reassure myself that everything was fine. *Okay, I'm kissing the guy I'd been flirting with... let's see where it goes.*

The next time wasn't so easy.

I was in bed, eyes still closed as I came back to my awareness one night. At first, I thought I'd just woken up in the middle of the night, the sheets cool to the touch as I lie on my back. I tried to rewind the tape in my mind to remind myself of the evening as I attempted to drift back to sleep. I'd been out at the bar singing karaoke with one of my best friends, Brittney, and her sister, Rachel. We met up with the guy I was dating, Jack, and his roommate. After bar close, we brought the party back to the guys' house. But then it all faded to black.

Nothing but a void remained in the place where the evening's events should have been. Annoyed by the absence and convinced I could manifest even a glimmer, I searched my memory for anything. Even one small hazy detail.

Suddenly, my mind was called to immediate attention as my body responded to a hand moving over my skin. Delicate fingers creeping up the inside of my thigh, skin on skin. Goosebumps spread across my legs in reflex to the touch while alarms sounded off in my head. *Come on, Kristy, remember. What's happening? I must still be with Jack.* The hand rose slowly, almost hesitantly, as Jack's voice broke through the silence. I couldn't tell what he said, but I knew immediately he wasn't talking to me.

My eyes shot open, and I pulled myself up onto my elbows to take in the scene. My blurred eyes came in to focus as I looked down at the foot of the bed, sharpening on Jack's confused expression. He was kneeling at the end of the bed naked. His eyes locked on mine, reflecting the dim light from the bedside lamp. Before I could let out a sigh of relief, my focus widened, and it became apparent were we were not alone. Poised next to Jack was Rachel, slowly retracting her hand from my bare thigh.

"Wha... wha... what the fuck is going on?" I tried to shout but I choked on the words as they tumbled out from my lips. I scrambled backward until I slammed into Jack's golden oak headboard, the thud so loud I thought it broke loose from the frame. Rachel, Brittney's nineteen-year-old sister, stared back at me with her big dark chocolate eyes. Her long, brown hair cascaded over her shoulders, covering her bare breasts. Confusion and apprehension swirled in her pupils.

Everyone spoke at once in rapid, clipped sentences, and I drew the covers up, hoping in some innocent way they would shield me from whatever was going on. I cowered there in the nude, desperate to understand what I had gotten myself into. "Somebody tell me what's going on!" I begged frantically.

"I thought you were into this," Jack backpedaled as Rachel covered herself with a pillow and shifted uncomfortably.

I clenched my eyes closed, shaking my head in disbelief. "Into what? No! Just... no! Rachel, get out!"

Mind racing and heart climbing into my throat, I continued shouting over the voices until Rachel grabbed a pile of clothes from the floor and fled the room. I tried to assemble the missing pieces, but my mind was still sloshing inside a pool of cheap beer. In my next breath, I grabbed at Jack and kissed him, desperate to regain control of the situation. I couldn't understand what had just happened. I couldn't make sense of how I got there and needed anything but silence in that moment. I was too afraid to close my eyes. Too fearful of being alone with my thoughts.

I found a beer on the nightstand and finished it in one gulp, turning off the lamp as I placed the empty vessel back on its perch. I pulled the blankets tighter around me and turned to Jack, "Can we just forget this ever happened?" He kissed me until my muscles eased and I relaxed enough to fall asleep, drifting off into a fitful slumber late into the night.

I walked out of Jack's room in the morning with my belongings in my hands, making shame-filled glances at the two sisters rising from their resting places on the sofas in the living room. The three of us girls had plans to have brunch with their mom, so we made our way outside to the sidewalk where she planned to pick us up. "How was your night?" she asked as we climbed into her minivan. Rachel and I mumbled responses like dismissive teenagers until Brittney blurted out from the seat next to me in back, "Rachel got invited to a threesome with Jack and Kristy!"

My jaw hit the floor.

"No, nothing happened," Rachel replied quickly in our defense.

A thick, silent pause filled the vehicle as I saw her mom glance back in the rearview mirror. "Are you upset that it wasn't you?" she asked earnestly and with unwavering ease, as if she was asking Brittney if she was sad she didn't make the volleyball team.

What? Those three had a relationship and open communication that I never could understand, but this conversation sailed way beyond my bounds of comprehension. "Yeah," Brittney responded with an obvious pang of disappointment in her voice. I couldn't speak. If this were TV, Brittney's statement would have been the punchline and some drink would have shot out of my nose as canned laughter lightened the mood. But in real life, the tension and disappointment filled the van like smoke, slowly swirling and spreading in the stillness. I leaned forward, pressing my forehead against the back of Rachel's seat. If only I could have shoved my pounding skull through the soft woven material, maybe then I could have escaped the moment all together.

Her mom laughed with more acceptance than I could fathom, and I withdrew from most of the conversations that followed. Brunch passed by in a fog as I held myself captive inside my thoughts. I was too embarrassed to admit I had no idea of how we got to that point or why I agreed to it at all. I was still a girl who thought sex in a car was salacious, let alone sex with guest appearances. I didn't speak to Jack for more than a week and our relationship quickly vanished into the same black void as my memories.

In recovery, flashbacks like these come back at inopportune times. Not the memory that was missing originally, no, that will never come back as it was never actually formed. But the memories of the aftermath come to me like ghosts appearing unexpectedly, lingering around in my periphery, reattaching themselves to me until I have the courage to look them in the face.

Some haunt me longer than others, demanding more of my time and attention, forcing me to sit with the memory of the girl or woman I once was. That's the sick thing about blackouts, about knowing there are alternate memories of me that exist out in the world. Things I have done, words I've said in anger or in love, feelings experienced but completely unknown to me. Pieces of me I will never know for myself.

Back then, it was easier to just walk away then ask the tough question: Had I come out of my blackout before things transpired between the three of us or had things already begun while I was blacked out? I took Rachel at her word that nothing happened. All that remains is learning how to come to terms with the parts I do remember. Those are the parts that left scars on my soul.

Not "Rock Bottom" Enough

The deepest hole ever dug is the Kola Well on the Kola Peninsula in Russia. It took teams of Soviet scientists almost twenty years to dig a record-breaking 40,230ft (approximately 8 miles or 1,147 school buses buried nose-to-nose below the surface of the earth). Years of broken equipment, disrupted funding, and site shut-downs impacted their speed but they eventually proved in 1989 as long as there is a way, the well will continue to get deeper (Bellows 2006).

Isn't that the same question in addiction? How far are you willing to dig before you stop?

Will you put down the shovel, or the bottle, before it kills you?

I grew up with an understanding that "rock bottom" only referred to the most extreme cases of addiction. The way it was kept in shadows, in secret, instilled in me the belief that recovery was only meant for people at the end of their rope.

The incarcerated, the homeless, the outcasts. As if you have to lose everything in order to become *worthy* of recovering.

Why do we force people trapped in addiction to wait and suffer before we deem them acceptable for getting help? Struggling up to the farthest reaches of human capacity in order to *earn the right* to change? We live in a society that values instant oatmeal and two-hour delivery. We want same-day service and on-demand viewing. Why delay recovery? Why deny them change when they need it? Or simply want it? What a fucking worthless societal rule.

I am a child of the eighties, raised in the Reagan era when First Lady Nancy Reagan led the fight against drugs and alcohol by championing D.A.R.E., Drug Abuse Resistance Education. It was taught in schools across America to teach kids to "Just say NO" to drugs and alcohol. I was in fifth grade when the program began and, as the perfectionist I was, I aimed to get it right.

They taught us LSD will drive you mad, cause you to jump out of a window to a tragic, unwelcome death.

*Okay, check, I will **not** be trying that.*

They taught us cocaine burned holes in your brain.

How was I supposed to maintain straight As with holes in my brain? I locked the decision to avoid it like law in my mind.

The lessons they taught us about alcohol were more dangerous because they were rooted on both sides of an invisible line. It was legal for adults, prohibited for children, found at most social events in life, yet dangerous. It reflected every way we looked at alcohol in one convoluted mash. We saw it at family gatherings and commercials on TV, yet the slideshow in Mrs. Voss's class focused on a homeless man with a scraggly beard and torn clothes. His toes peeked out of one boot as he drank from a bottle concealed by a paper bag. The same type of paper bag that housed a peanut butter and jelly sandwich stowed away inside my desk.

They taught us to "just say NO," but nothing about what happens in between saying "yes" and realizing "I've gone too far." Where were the beer-guzzling college kids and executives drinking bourbon? Images of mommy-wine culture and party dads? Anything we could possibly see in ourselves before it ever became too late.

I held that picture of rock bottom in my mind like a guidepost, one I'd strive to never venture beyond. Thinking to myself as I drank over the years, *As long as I can keep my shit together, I'll be alright.* Later in life, staring at my reflection with bloodshot eyes, nauseous and wiping at the smeared mascara, I never saw the image of the man at rock bottom. Never saw a woman worthy of getting help.

My vision of rock bottom became just another rule that hurt more than kept me safe. *I'll only drink on weekends. I'll know when to stop.* I felt ashamed to admit to anyone I was in too deep, in way over my head. I was so convinced I wasn't worthy, I just kept digging, reaching farther than I ever wanted to go.

* * *

After that night with Jack and Rachel, I was spooked. The night had exploded for all of us, and for me, created an internal rock slide of worry and self-loathing that took me out at the knees. I was too afraid to admit it had gotten out of control and too ashamed to ask how it all transpired. All I knew was I had somehow wandered into territory where I didn't feel safe, and I wasn't going to feign that I was comfortable with any of it. I never spoke about it again, not with Jack, nor Rachel. We just went on pretending it never happened.

Soon after, Jack stopped calling me to hang out on the weekends. It took only a couple weeks to realize he only called me after bar close any more. All I desired was to find a companion, to be cared for, but it seemed all he ever wanted was a booty call. It became treacherous ground to walk on that exploded in one drunken phone call. Burning hot with whiskey on my tongue, I screamed at him through the phone until my tears ran dry and a silent hush fell over the line.

I felt cheap and used, discarded like I meant nothing at all to him. I heard him breathing and didn't have a fuck left to give for any response he had. The fact that he listened, that I ever had the guts to say it all, left me feeling like the fire burning inside had been extinguished.

"Don't call me," I said forcefully then hung up the phone.

But the landslide had just begun.

I continued meeting my friends at our regular bar just blocks from Jack's place. Three, four nights a week we met up for beers and karaoke. We just found a new table for my girlfriends and me to hang out at. I still couldn't reconcile my feelings about that night, so I began drinking heavier, attempting to drive them all away.

Later that summer, I was invited to a backyard BBQ that my college classmate, Karl, was hosting for his roommate's birthday. Karl hung out at the bar too and had always hated Jack. I brushed him off. The curtains that hid his true reasons parted in the wind and exposed his secrets when he'd mix in his own requests to take me out on a date. But he was a nice guy and what good girl wouldn't want to join a sunny, late summer party with friends?

I had no intention to stay the night at Karl's or wind up at Jack's apartment just a few blocks over. To maintain control, I held myself to four glasses of beer with the intent to drive myself home after sobering up. *Yeah, the liver can handle one beer an hour, so I should be good.* It had started to rain at sunset and the party moved indoors. A few people headed home, but I still needed time to sober up, so I hung around with the last handful of friends. Some couples retreated together to the couch or to open bedrooms to make out, and I tried to stay out of their way. Karl offered me his room for the night but something inside of me insisted *No.* I was running low on trust at the time and took a blanket so I could curl myself into a ball on an old club chair in the living room.

I slept intermittently for a few hours, waking a few times to sounds of the couples sucking face on the couch across the room. I woke again sometime after 3:00 a.m. to a booming thunderstorm outside, noticing the amorous couple had finally fallen asleep. Looking at my watch, I thought to myself, *I have been sleeping for four hours... I'm okay to drive myself home.* I snuck out without disturbing the other passed-out partiers, got in my emerald green car, and headed home.

The rain exploded on my windshield like water balloons, smearing my vision so fast the wipers couldn't keep pace. The headlights reflected off the soaked highway, and I felt steady as I navigated my way home. Before I could react, the car hydroplaned as I crossed a low section of road and spun 180 degrees at highway speed. The car slid off the road, coming to rest in the tall grass of the median between the north and southbound lanes. I sat stunned with my hands still on the wheel. The engine idled in drive but went nowhere, the wipers swinging across the windshield, now completely covered in mud from the slide into the grass. Each stroke exposed a little more of the median before me.

"Fuck."

At this time in the world, all I had with me was an analog cellphone that could store ten of my favorite phone numbers. As it turned out, I hadn't chosen our trusted hometown tow company to put on my top-ten list. I put the car in park but left it running so I could stay warm while I figured out what to do. It was probably two miles to the nearby Perkins, the only place open at that hour, but I didn't feel like making the trek on foot in the rain.

Still thinking I did nothing wrong, I did the most logical thing I could think of...

I called 911.

On myself.

Because I thought I was *sober enough* to have driven home.

I was either that dumb or that drunk. Likely a mix of both. But in all honesty, I was so confident I had given myself enough time to sober up that I thought I was doing the smart thing.

I thought I could call and request assistance from the Highway Helpers, a program that comes out to help clear minor incidents from the highways to prevent further congestion or problems. Unfortunately, the dispatcher sent a state trooper instead. I turned the wipers off while I waited for help to arrive, having promised to stay in the car.

Soon after, the trooper arrived, knocking on my window with his flashlight. I rolled down the window as rain fell from the brim of his campaign hat. "Are you doing okay? Can you tell me what happened?" I explained the hydroplaning and losing control, blaming it on my bald tires, unaware I could still be drunk.

"Have you been drinking?" he asked calmly.

"I only had a few beers last night, but not since 11:00 p.m." It was now after three in the morning. *Totally enough time to burn it all off,* I thought to myself.

"Please step out of the car," he said, stepping back to make room so I could exit.

I passed the field sobriety test, somehow capable of walking a straight line in my three-inch heels on the shoulder of the highway in the rain. There was no fooling the breathalyzer test. I failed on the first try and the trooper kindly led me to the back seat of his squad car. He was a compassionate man, one who may have even had a daughter my age. He never berated me or intimidated me over the horrible thing I had done. Maybe it was something in my eyes, but whatever it was, whoever he was, he was sympathetic and made me feel safe.

I stared at my car in silence from the backseat of the squad car as the rain washed down the windows like condensation on a beer glass as he stood outside and called for a tow truck. With only the sound of the heat pumping through the vents, a thought flitted up from deep down, an echo from inside a well.

Tonight was the most sober I have driven home all week.

* * *

I had just turned twenty-two years old, fresh out of a night in jail and about to walk into my first AA meeting a few days later. My dad hadn't spoken to me since he bailed me out, but I wasn't at all surprised. I easily read the disgust on his face as the guard released me from my cell to meet him and my stepmom in the lobby. The continuous cold shoulder at home eliminated any hope I had of ever being forgiven.

Jenny had come up with the idea for trying an AA meeting and offered to come with me for support. She had left the party earlier that night and was exactly the friend I needed at that point in my life.

The only meeting in our small suburban town was in the basement of one of the seven Lutheran churches. My license had been immediately revoked when I blew double the legal limit back at the station, so I arrived at the church door by bicycle. We walked in together and timidly followed a few people down the stairs to a large room in the basement. Slate grey metal folding chairs were lined in rows, and tiny windows on one wall let the afternoon sun leak in and mix with the florescent lights overhead. We found two spots in the back row and took a seat.

God grant me the serenity...

The meeting began in prayer, and I listened politely to the words I didn't know. Both of my parents were raised Catholic but neither stuck with the religion. Dad raised me atheist and said I could pick any religion I wanted. Mom never really gave up searching for the right one for her. Over the years, I had sung in Baptist churches and fought through sleepy head-bobbing during Catholic masses. I was baptized Lutheran with my siblings when they were still infants then, years later, tried accepting Jesus at the nondenominational church my friends attended. No matter where I went, or who dragged me there, none of them ever gave me that sense of calm and belonging I always expected church should make you feel. This was no different. I fidgeted slightly in my chair in discomfort.

The only things I had known about AA prior to stepping through those doors were the pictures painted for me within school walls and hushed conversations. Meetings were the place addicts met to come clean about the horrible things they had done while intoxicated by drink. Such degenerates, no one spoke of their problem outside the meeting. It was too dark, too taboo to speak of in polite society. I didn't know anyone who went to AA or had recovered from alcohol. For all I knew, no one had a problem with alcohol. No one but me.

In a town this small, everyone in that room was some classmate's mother, a neighbor, even the cashier at the grocery store I saw every Friday. I was wary about the true anonymity within those walls and, when it came time, neither Jenny nor I volunteered to speak. I watched as people stood up front and told stories from the darkest haunts of their memories. I could identify with the lighthearted jokes about another hangover, but "I am an alcoholic" was not a statement I could identify with. I wasn't ready to accept the label of some disease without a better understanding of what I was going through.

Back then, there were "alcoholics" and there were "normal" people. It was a disease you were born with and yet there were no genetic markers to identify as the cause. Neither of my parents were big drinkers, and it was rarely around either house. I wasn't the hopeless derelict that had nothing to lose, I just drank to have fun. It didn't make sense. *What if I'm not an "alcoholic" and still need help?*

We sat like statues in the back of the room as we listened to stories of broken homes and divorce: A woman's tearful retelling of vodka bottles hidden in nooks and crannies around her home. Traumatized adults whose families no longer spoke to them. Recognizable tales of trembling hands and mornings spent heaving bile into a toilet. They flayed themselves out on the podium at the front of the room, most finishing their stories with the mournful regret that they'd never get to drink again. Something within that sentiment made me want to drink more.

After the meeting ended, people mingled outside on the church's front step. A woman in her late forties with skin aged well beyond its years introduced herself as Ricki. We gave her our names along with a shy response about my DUI that led us there that day. I anticipated a welcome acceptance and support from the stranger, some recognition of my fear and apprehension. Instead, I was smacked in the face with judgment and dismissal.

"Oh, kid. One DUI is not 'bottom.' Let me guess, you still live with your parents, right? Did they kick you out?" she squeezed out a layer of snark so thick it felt like I could reach out, grab it, and slap the smirk right off her face with it.

"No," I forced out of my clenched jaw, feeling my power drain out of my body.

"Lose your job?"

My eyes dropped in dismay. "No."

"Keep drinking, kid. Then, come back when you've really fucked up." She turned and walked away.

"What?" I looked at Jenny incredulously as I pulled her toward the parking lot. "But I could have killed someone! What an... an... AA-hole!" I snapped in a hushed tone as people drank brown-flavored water and mingled nearby. Like the beginning of my relationship with alcohol, I was trying to find a connection. But even here, at a meeting full of people admittedly addicted to alcohol, a group I thought would understand my shame and powerlessness, I wasn't "rock bottom" enough. Not worthy of their club. *Just keep drinking until it gets worse.*

Jenny and I parted ways after that first meeting ended. She in her parents' Jeep and me on my bicycle. She went home and I, dejected and even more confused, rode my bike straight to the nearest bar. I took a seat on a torn stool in the dimly lit room and ran through the meeting in my head while I clutched a pint of beer.

What the fuck is wrong with you, Kristy? I sat quietly and thumbed the condensation on my glass, creating cascading drops that ran to the drink napkin stuck to the base. Like the rain on the squad car windows, they fell in crooked streams that mirrored my hopes. The cold reminded me of the metal slat I slept on that night in jail. Wearing only a tank top and shorts that summer night, one of the female guards gave me a prisoner jacket to curl up in as I tried to sleep away my reality. *Isn't AA supposed to help you quit?*

At the next meeting, they gave away free copies of "the Big Book," *Alcoholics Anonymous,* that explained their beliefs about alcoholism and a *Twelve Steps* booklet outlining how to work through their program. I thumbed through them, choking on the overarching masculinity on the pages. Phrases like "we are like men who" and "drink like a gentleman" gave way to chapters with names like "To Wives" that made me gag (Wilson 2001). In step one of the *Twelve Steps,* I read more on how insistent they were for everyone to first reach rock bottom: "Why all this insistence that every A.A. must hit bottom first? ... the average alcoholic, self-centered in the extreme, doesn't care for this prospect—unless he has to do these things in order to stay alive himself" (Wilson 2021).

After three meetings, I stopped going. The "true alcoholics" didn't think I belonged there. Who was I to beg for their acceptance?

* * *

In the next six months, I was sober mostly due to lack of resources. I was still living with my dad, and with no driver's license, I was limited to class and school for reasons to get myself out of the house each day. At family gatherings and holidays, I felt like an outcast, too afraid to have a drink with the rest of them as if everyone would instantly judge me. During that time, most of the people I thought were friends disappeared too. Like pebbles tossed down a well, they dropped out of sight. Nothing but the faint echo of them remained as they vanished into the darkness below.

The aftermath of my DUI had left me feeling trapped in a constant state of uncertainty and shame where I was too afraid to even look anyone in the eye any longer. After a month, my driver's license was reinstated but only as a permit to drive myself to work and school. There were designated hours I could drive and specific, direct routes I was allowed to navigate to keep myself from returning to jail. I had special plates on the car to notify the highway patrol they could pull me over and breathalyze me for no reason at all. No matter how great an exam score I received, how much I made in tips each night, walking out to see those plates shattered every ounce of happiness I found. Every fucking time.

It was around that time I met Bruce, a friend of a coworker I met while we played pool after waiting tables one night. Bruce had a steady calm about him that was warm and welcoming. He was also a child of divorced and remarried parents, one side that drank heavily and another that lived by the teachings of AA. He was stuck somewhere between the sober side and the drinking one, trying to love everyone without having to plant his flag on one side or another. I appreciated having someone who understood the dark landscape of having to form parental alliances to survive. Somehow I liked that he came with his own booze-lined baggage.

His only ask was that I would stay sober while we were together. It seemed like an easy concession to make, and at the time, he seemed like the only person willing to accept the idea of me quitting alcohol exactly where I was. I never shared the details that led up to my DUI with him or his sober family, the ones making it so easy to attempt a sober life. They never asked, rather just guided and encouraged me as I learned to take it one day at a time.

I moved in with him quickly and I learned how to stay dry from his sober parents. We avoided most social events I would typically drink at, which honestly, was all of them. We stuck together at weddings and funerals like cliques at a school dance, traveling in pairs or not at all. I was always looking back over my shoulder at the people singing, dancing, and embracing one another with drink in hand. Tugged to the edge of the party by abstinence while trying to inhale the magic pixie dust in the air. As if drinking still held the key to another layer of experiencing life. Everything revolved around the doctrine that "alcoholics never truly recover." I couldn't help but think, *If you can't recover then what's the point?*

At one year sober, Bruce's stepdad gave me a one-year AA token. "Good job, kid," he smiled with his large jolly grin as he pulled me into his tall frame for a celebratory hug. We sat on swivel chairs in front of his kitchen picture window as he told me the story about the coin. It was his one-year token from when he had gotten sober decades before. I admired the freshly shined bronze coin as I turned it over in my hand. I kept it in my pocket for many years, thumbing it when I was around alcohol, trying to feel each letter to take my mind off the drink I couldn't have.

Over the next three years, being sober helped me finish college but I slowly became a muted version of myself. An illusion. Back then, I found it was easier to not think of alcohol if I didn't venture out into the world. I didn't go out with my friends, quit the book club I had loved for years, and made excuses to my family so I could stay home. It was easier to avoid everything than to try to not drink some nights, never knowing which nights would make me crave another glass.

Depressed, disinterested in doing anything I loved, I was going through the motions to get from day to day.

One morning, I sat down at my computer with a cup of coffee after Bruce stepped out for a few hours. I began typing in a website name into the browser, but an incorrectly typed letter caused it to recommend a site I didn't know. The URL name alluded to something about attractive singles and my suspicion piqued. I hit enter to follow the suggested site, landing on a home page of provocative women and Bruce's email address saved in the login field. The password was empty, and I began to fume as I realized it was a hook-up site, a way to search for sexual escapades with strangers nearby.

I confronted him when he returned home, feeling betrayed and heartbroken by a man I thought I would eventually marry. He attempted to convince me it was "just to look at pictures while masturbating." When I paired that with the surprisingly empty box of condoms in our night stand I had noticed weeks before, I no longer knew what to believe.

He sat on the edge of the sofa as I perched on a kitchen stool across the room. I demanded he find somewhere to go the next morning so I could pack up my belongings and leave. It was just another point in my life where I wasn't enough for someone I trusted and thought I loved. Now it was time to leave.

"Face it: there's no such thing as Hollywood romances, Kristy. No one will ever put you on a pedestal," he scowled defensively as he sat back and crossed his arms. The back of the counter dug into my skin, and I leaned back harder, embracing the pain. The ache distracted me for a moment as I channeled my rage for strength, willing it to swell and flow like molten lava up from my feet and into my chest. The heat erupted, melting the walls I built around my heart so I could harness the truth about the life I wanted. One I thought I deserved.

I may have been a child of divorced parents who struggled to see her place in this world, but they still taught me to believe in true love. Cosmic, mystical soulmates destined to be together. I believed there was joy to be found and meaning to explore. I believed there was some soul-fueling future for myself somehow, that dream safely protected behind the walls I built around my heart.

"I'm willing to find out," I countered, my eyes narrowed and sharp.

I left the room and began packing, making good on my promise and leaving my key as I moved out the very next day.

It wasn't long after I left Bruce that I made the decision to start drinking again. I had withdrawn from all the people and places I loved to protect myself from the longing I still carried for booze. But alcohol is in every celebration, ceremony, and ritual we know: weddings, funerals, birthdays, and baby showers. Baby showers! Where the guests of honor, mom, and baby, are unable to drink yet all the attendees mark it as the perfect occasion for mimosas and bloody Mary's. I didn't want to keep living a life of avoidance. I wanted to live in *my* world with the people I loved.

After more than three years sober, I believed there was solid evidence I finally had control over alcohol and myself. But the truth was, like any good drilling team, I had really just decided to stop digging for a spell. I imagine the drilling teams on the Kola Peninsula asked themselves, "Do we keep digging?" many times over the years. Had they stopped, they never would have accomplished a world record like they did.

There have been many times in my life that I had asked myself if I had hit rock bottom. Like most people struggling with addiction, I just kept thinking, *I'm not that bad.* Each time it simply proved there was always another level to dig myself down into. The Kola project was eventually abandoned when a drill became stuck in the rock and teams were unable to get it moving again. Eventually, it got to the point where my inner voice begged for something to tell me to stop digging.

Sometimes, just sometimes, I wonder to myself...
Did I need to keep digging in order to break through what kept me entombed all along?

Pedestal

––––

The summer after I left Bruce, I was determined to find myself. Scratch that... recreate myself. I had spent so much time homebound and bottled up, avoiding my friends and family simply to avoid the possibility of drinking alcohol after promising him I would abstain. All of that was over, along with the main reason I had leaned on to stay sober. A fresh start was needed in order to restore some understanding of myself and explore aspects of life I'd never known. There was a magical life out there for me to find; I merely had to look in places I hadn't yet searched.

I set a goal to try new things each week like belly dancing and yoga, joining a gym and registering to run a 5K. Dinners with loved ones filled my body with savory new foods, devouring the flavors along with the energy that reinvigorated between us. I felt alive each time I saw them and affirmed I was back on the right path of living a life out with the rest of the world. Yet, no matter how many times I tried to embrace time with myself, I was still uncomfortable with the thoughts I carried around.

I'm an adult now. I can handle myself. I negotiated with myself about how far I had come, how steady I was, obviously stable enough to return to drinking. *Just with dinner, when I'm out with my friends. A glass of wine here and there can't hurt.* The next chapter began.

I was obsessed with the movie *Under the Tuscan Sun* at the time, watching Diane Lane's transformation every Friday night from my temporary home in my dad and stepmom's basement. In the film, the heroine goes through an unexpected divorce and her world completely unravels. Her friends send her off to Italy on a bicycle wine tour, urging her to rediscover her light amidst all her despair. I saw so much of myself in her. The lines between the life I thought I'd been living and the truth had crossed and twisted so much, I felt I no longer knew who I was. As she untwisted herself in the movie, I realized I required an equally massive effort to restore the ties with myself.

"I need to go to Italy," I said one night as the credits rolled for the umpteenth time. Sitting back on my bed, I grabbed my journal and started to plot out my adventure. *First, I'll need a bike.* A coworker had a picture of herself on a fancy bike at work; she would be the perfect person to ask.

Once Monday came, I stopped at Vicki's desk with some contracts to sign and gestured to the framed photo. "Do you still ride bikes?" I asked, taking in the mountain bike she was riding in the picture. She nodded and reminisced about her race victory that day. "Do you know a good shop to go to if I'm looking to buy a bike for myself?" I asked, selfishly collecting intel for the plan brewing in my mind.

She grabbed a pen and paper, quickly jotting down a number. "This is the place you want to go. He's the best," she said as she handed over the note. I turned it toward me to find only the word "Hollywood" and a number to call.

It echoed in my head like a whisper, and I looked at her confused, "What's his name?"

"Mitch. But everyone calls him Hollywood."

I had spent months working to reconnect with myself after leaving Bruce but, in that moment, I heard his voice crystal clear in my mind. "There's no such thing as a Hollywood romance. No one will ever put you on a pedestal." I laughed to myself at the memory then brushed it off with a tiny shake of my head.

I called the shop a few days later and set up an appointment for a bike fitting with the owner. When I arrived, I was greeted by a man with salt-and-pepper hair lounging in a director's chair. "I'm here to see Hollywood about a bike. I'm Kristy," I said as I took in the trophies and trinkets on the walls.

"That's me. Hi, I'm Mitch. Right this way," he motioned as he rose and walked to the back of the store. He had a bicycle already built for me and ready to try out that day, but it took a few appointments for us to get all the measurements right. I wanted a bicycle I could explore the Italian countryside on, and he refused to send a customer out the door without a custom fitting for every bike.

He was confident and animated, lighting up as he explained all the ways the bike would meet my needs. We sat together in the back talking about our favorite rock bands and concerts, sports, and things you can fix DIY. The conversation flowed easily, splashing joyfully over shared interests and unbelievable tales. "The only thing I've ever caught fly fishing was a dragonfly," I said dramatically.

He smiled and looked me in the eye, "You're part dude, aren't you?" I laughed knowingly, having been called a tomboy my entire life. I was impressed on how well he read me in so little time.

We became fast friends and, before I knew it, I was falling head over heels in love. The night he asked me out, I knew it in every inch of my body that there was something different about him. My body thrummed with warmth and ease when I was near him, a sanctuary where I was free to be myself. I got lost in his cocoa eyes and felt his energy shoot through me every time he grabbed my hand.

Mitch introduced me to new friends and the welcoming bike community in town. We had a shared passion for live music and the great outdoors. Everything just clicked. He invited me on a European bike tour he and a friend were hosting six months later and I enthusiastically signed up, pivoting my Italian adventure for France and Belgium. I didn't believe he had fallen as hard for me until he got down on one knee. Next to the Lake of Love in Bruges, Belgium, during a horse-drawn carriage ride, Mitch stopped to ask me to marry him.

"Kristy Kreme, you're my everything. Will you marry me?"

"Shut the fuck up! You're kidding." Staring into his teary eyes while a swan swam alongside us quizzically, the words stumbled out before I could stop them.

His smile stretched wider as he shook his head, and my hands began to tremble as I delicately placed them on his cheeks. "Yes! YES!" I giggled as passersby cheered in celebration. My "Hollywood romance" was real and as vibrant as the green color of leaves after a lightning storm. It was electric and breathed fresh life into me as I sat jubilantly perched on the pedestal built by Mitch.

I moved in with him when we returned from our trip, and we became inseparable. He saw the real me, the awkward, goofy, playful me, and didn't run away. But, where that sincere affection should have reassured me, it began to deteriorate into worry instead. As love and acceptance coursed through my veins, so did the terror of losing it all. Losing him. As my insecurities mushroomed, I drank more heavily to try to bury them all away. To disguise my imperfections, my weaknesses. My fractured joists.

What started out as wine with dinner on special nights and beers out at concerts on Tuesdays, rolled into multiple bottles of wine at my new book club and at movie night with the girls. It was screwdrivers at breakfast and midday naps when I got too drunk on weekends, shaking off hangovers every day in between.

Mitch put me on the pedestal and treated me like a queen, never asking me to quit or questioning if things had derailed far enough. He called me "Boozie the Clown" and picked me up if I stumbled. He never asked me to drive home. He saw the beloved woman he had hoisted up there while I tried to block his eyes from the parts of me I was too scared to reveal. I thought his love could save me, held on to it as if it could replace the love I didn't feel for myself. I thought my happy life would protect me from falling, but the more dependent on alcohol I became, the more I teetered at the top.

* * *

I wonder if we, as a society, can ever take alcohol down from the pedestal it rules from. The way it's expected to be present at every social gathering and venue. We raise our glasses in ceremony and rely on it to soothe the deepest sorrows bound to loss and grief. It's supposed to make us feel sexy and desirable, confident and free. It's extremely dangerous and highly illegal to drink and drive, yet beer brands are emblazoned on race cars and team apparel all over the country. To say it's engrained in our society is an understatement.

Kids driving you crazy? How about a nice glass of merlot in a closet for a bout of self-care?

Wife nagging you? Cold beer in the garage.

Parents embarrassing you? Go steal vodka shots in the den.

Husband ignoring you? Wine, popcorn, and romcoms. And tissues, don't forget the tissues.

Alcohol addiction can lead to depression, anxiety, tremors, cancer, liver disease, delirium, and suicide. And blackouts.

As a drinker's consumption increases over time, so does their tolerance, increasing the amount needed to feel the same effect. But the hippocampus in the brain, the part responsible for creating long-term memories, is incapable of building up tolerance (Scaccia 2023). Your brain, arguably the most important organ, cannot adapt to the increased consumption of ethanol. As the blood-alcohol levels continue to rise, the brain eventually just stops transferring the data to protect itself. The moments vanishing as if they never happened. Poof! Gone.

But we rely on it for its familiarity and the way we believe it cures our ails. Alcohol rests so high up on that pedestal that, in spite of the possible side effects, some scientists strive to master moderation. Those researchers are still in pursuit of the magic way to help people addicted to alcohol drink with control. What if, instead, we said, "Hey, Lucy. This just isn't for you. It's okay, go enjoy the sober living!"

When we put things on a pedestal, they become an idol. Something of admiration and worship, completely void of faults. But that's the thing about alcohol: there's not one, perfectly safe drink out there for everyone. Taking it down is the only way we can destigmatize sobriety, addiction, and living alcohol-free.

It wasn't until I could see alcohol for what it truly was that I was able to take it down off the pedestal I set it on, too.

* * *

Six years into marriage and things were still splendid with Mitch and me. We traveled often and filled our cameras with pictures of breathtaking sunsets and stunning views. But somehow, even with the boundless affection and amazing life we built, the ground continued to give way beneath me. Alcohol continued to drag me down. No matter how wonderful my life was, I still carried around all those insecurities, doubt, and self-hate. I shoved them in my suitcase and dragged them everywhere I went.

We road-tripped to Louisville, KY, for the first ever World Championship Cyclo-cross Race held on US soil. Cyclo-cross, a Belgian-born discipline of bicycle racing, is raced on courses made of dirt, mud, and grass. The bikes resemble road bikes with treaded tires and the course is full of tight turns, technical descents, and obstacles that force the rider to jump off their bike and run. Hands down, it's the most spectator-friendly bike racing around. We were over the moon about getting to watch the best in the world compete only a twelve-hour drive from home.

It was January, so Mitch got us huge matching t-shirts to throw on over our winter gear to make us easier to find in the crowd. In one of his sleeves, he had a rolled-up sign with his shop's logo so he could do some guerilla marketing, knowing there would be multiple cameras on course for the world broadcast. We stayed in our travel trailer at a nearby campground for the three-day event, keeping ourselves warm with a tiny ceramic heater when the temps dipped below fifteen degrees Fahrenheit at night. A blizzard on our first night shut down the town, cancelled schools the next day, and even halted the pizza delivery drivers. We made the most of it with some Minnesotan friends who caravanned with us, laughing at the snow we wouldn't even shovel back home as we grilled burgers outside.

The blizzard was just one of many recent winter storms that had affected the area in recent weeks. We woke the next morning to an updated event schedule from the promoter notifying everyone all the events were going to be mashed into one long Saturday of races. The course that hosted the event was on a low-lying section along the Ohio River which had now risen to record levels. Dikes were constructed around the entire park to hold the rushing waters at bay long enough to crown the new World Champions.

The high temp for the day was supposed to rise to the low forties, so we bundled up in insulated overalls and winter jackets for a long day of spectating. The promoter must have been surprised when more than ten thousand people flocked there from all over the US and Europe because there was only one tent with four lines to serve all the beer and food. My friends and I bitched and moaned about how long it took to get a beer and how much racing we missed while refueling. But seeing the greatest racers in the world compete in our favorite sport was worth every inconvenience.

As the temps rose, the snow melted, devolving the entire course into slippery, wet mud. Spectators slipped and stumbled as they traversed the slick park, and we cheered as muddy racers slid and passed one another in the treacherous conditions. Mitch and I split from our friends for the main event so he could focus on where the cameras were and get his sign on TV as often as possible. I stood by his side, anxious to grab another beer before the big show.

"I'm gonna run and grab a beer quick. Do you want anything?" I added the offer as if it would prevent him from objecting to my plan.

"Whatever you do, don't go over that hill," he said, pointing at a steep muddy hill near us. "You're gonna slip and get covered in mud and we have to get in Jim's truck to get back to camp. Don't. Go. Over. That. Hill."

I nodded and stuck my tongue out playfully as I walked off toward the beer tent already five or six drinks into my day.

As I made my trek across the park to the concessions, I crossed paths with three men in luchador wrestling masks carrying a case of beer. I complimented them on their look, not at all out of place for a sport that frequently brought out spectators in costumes. "Where did you score a whole case?" I asked as I pointed to the beer. One of the masked strangers pulled out a can and offered it to me. To show my gratitude, I stayed for a few minutes as we traded predictions for the race along the rising river, enjoying the hoppy flavor of my score.

Remember that part about tolerance and the brain? There's no warning, no caution flag to tell you it's coming until, suddenly, everything goes blank.

That beer put me over the edge, barreling straight into a blackout in the middle of a wonderful, sunny day. The next thing I knew, I was stumbling up the same muddy hill Mitch warned me about, hearing him call to me from off in the distance. I stood in place once I saw him, wasted and swaying from side to side. He looked me over, obviously annoyed by my grubby appearance. "I told you not to go down that hill!" I followed his eyes as he took in the greasy mud that covered me from head to toe.

"I slipped," was the only excuse I could come up with.

I followed him back to our friend's truck with uneven steps and a whirlpool of guilt roiling inside of me. I discarded my muddy jacket and snow pants, turning them inside-out and tossing them into the bed of the truck, then piled inside once the others arrived. I was a wasted little imp who missed the entire race, yet Mitch helped clean me up and got me a cheeseburger on our drive back to camp to try to soak up some of the beer. He tucked me in back at our campsite so I could nap it off and went on like usual as we reconvened around the campfire later that night with our friends.

The next evening, Mitch found an internet replay of the race that we could stream on our laptop in our cozy home away from home. *Perfect*, I thought to myself, *now I can see what I missed*. What did Shakespeare say? "Something wicked this way comes?"

I poured myself a glass of wine and crawled into bed next to him, pulling the covers up to ward off the chilly winter air outside. Our mini dachshund, Rosco, laid across my feet warming my toes. Mitch pulled up the pro women's race on my laptop and I sipped my merlot as we watched every minute, cheering and commentating along with all the action.

We pointed and shouted like kids playing "I Spy" each time we saw Mitch peeking out from crowd, flashing his sign for the cameras as the leaders rode near him on course. "There you are!" I would giggle and point at the small screen, beaming with pride for him.

Glimpses of me by his side were revealed in a few camera shots as we mixed in with the crowd of rowdy revelers that lined every inch of the course. Once the men's race began, we saw how Mitch made his way to the best vantage points to ensure he got on camera during the main event. We delighted and counted each time we saw him, snuggling together under the warm blankets as I took in the race I missed. Missed because I was searching for alcohol instead.

A few laps before the men's race ended, I noticed Mitch in the crowd but this time he wasn't holding up his sign. The static camera stayed on a technical, muddy feature as the racers came through, throngs of fans screaming for their favorite teams. But not Mitch. His head turned from side to side, scanning the crowd rather than watching the race. A telltale sign of searching for something, or *someone*, in a sea of ten thousand muddy fans. My heart sunk so fast in my chest I swore the thud echoed off the camper walls. It broke on impact, a piercing pain that swept through me as I clutched the wine glass in my hand.

A few camera changes later, there I was, leaned up against one of the dikes as the river raged just inches away. Just me, a beer, and three men in wrestling masks as if we were old friends catching up over drinks. We were both silent as we listened to the post-race recaps and watched the cameras toggle through every angle of the course, showcasing the droves of fans from across the globe. We saw Mitch one more time, stomping through the mud and weaving through the hordes, still obviously searching for me.

My eyes stayed glued to the screen, too terrified of possibly seeing a pained look on his face. There I was, Boozie the Clown, unmasked on screen for all to see. Watching him look for me, this man who loved me for better or worse, through the good, bad, and ugly, while I was off giving all my time and attention to booze. Watching it play out on screen devastated me.

I dropped my face into my hands and sighed out a desperate apology. "Shit, honey, I'm so sorry." I knew the words did nothing to erase my behavior that day. I had gone off and did my own thing, caring nothing for how it impacted the love of my life. On our vacation. I wandered off to fill my need to drink. In that moment, I wasn't worried if he would forgive me because I hated myself enough for the two of us.

Mitch half laughed it off, but there was a deep layer of annoy-ance in his voice. "You were such a pill," he joked lightly as he looked over at me. I sat unblinking as the reality of it all set in. I had everything I could dream of for my life. I had it all, but I kept drinking as if I was trying to throw it all away.

He forgave me. He always did. But this time, I couldn't for-give myself. For the first time, I could see just how far I had fallen from the pedestal he built especially for me. It was a love I didn't feel I deserved. Eventually, he would have to see it too.

* * *

I wrote this chapter one night from a plush grey chair in the living room as Mitch watched football from the sofa nearby. "How come you never asked me to stop drinking? Why didn't you say anything?" I asked him earnestly during a commercial break.

The look on his face was soft as he turned to me with a tender smile. "I have known guys who couldn't get out of the house in the morning without a mug of straight vodka to start the day." He rolled into stories of friends so trapped in addiction, so heavily sedated, they would urinate in jars in their bedrooms before using the bathroom down the hall. Friends on multi-day benders getting fired for not showing up to work. "They couldn't function without it. You never got that bad."

With the people we love, it can be hard to see the truth behind the fantasy. The reality that hides behind the potential we imagine. His love couldn't make me better, couldn't heal the growing addiction, the slow dimming of the light inside me. But the display of his love gave me something to fight for. It reminded me I might be someone worth living for after all.

Piss in Boots

"What did you just do?" Mitch blurted out as he flipped the switch, flooding our bedroom with light in the middle of the night.

"What are you talking about? You just woke me up!" I said defensively, rubbing at my eyes. I squinted as I searched his face for clues to what was going on.

"Follow me," he said as he motioned me to join him in the other room. Strangely, I noticed he was holding one of his winter boots in his hand as we navigated the short pathway through our tiny kitchen into the bathroom.

He pulled back the shower curtain and held his boot over the drain and tipped it over. I watched with confusion as some unknown liquid poured from his boot. Once it dwindled down into the last final drips, Mitch looked back at me expecting an answer.

I had no clue what was happening. *What the hell is in your boot, Mitch?*

"You pissed in my boot!"

* * *

Mitch and I returned home one night after attending a Sunday dinner at my dad and stepmom's home. My Iowa-born husband had quickly adapted to our very Minnesotan traditions around meals. Family dinners were usually warm, inviting, and brimming with comfort. There was always way too much food, you eat more than you ever would at home, and almost always need a nap soon after. Conversations in Minnesota are light and hover safely at surface level, typically focusing on the weather, road construction, sports, food, and yes, more weather.

This night was different. Somewhere in between the complex lives we were living and the things that always went unsaid, I could feel a buzz of tension rising in my limbs, my nerve endings twitching and firing as I stared at my plate. Something in the idle conversation that night fed my insecurities deep inside. An angry monster, hiding in the darkness, telling me no one really wanted me there. To drown the jilted troll who snarled from within me, I kept drinking until it shut up.

One goblet of heavily poured wine followed another until my lips and teeth turned purple and my ass molded into the dining room chair. I drank to hold my feelings captive and hasten my tongue, keeping it busy with swallowing until the wine no longer had flavor. I kept pouring until it came time to say our goodbyes and bottle up my emotions yet again.

Mitch drove us home that night as he always did; my handler, husband, and "sober cab," or "designated driver" as it's known elsewhere. Once safe in the dark shadows of our small condo, I grabbed my indestructible acrylic wine glass and a box of red wine. Holding down the nozzle, I bitched aloud about all the things I had wanted to say that night and didn't. I drank almost to the point of passing out before stumbling off to bed, arms outstretched toward every table and dresser that I passed along the way. I hoisted myself into bed and immediately drifted off once I turned out the lights, frustrated tears drying on the sides of my face.

Somewhere in the middle of the night, my coma-like slumber was frantically interrupted by Mitch and the painfully bright lights that filled the room. The sodden boot being poured into the shower drain gave me no insight to what had transpired, so I stared at him with confusion tattooed across my face.

"You pissed in my boot!" he said with his own haze of disbelief.

"I did what?" The accusation was preposterous. There was no way that was true. I watched as he reached in and turned on the shower, washing the evidence down the drain. *Why would I pee in his boot? I was just sleeping a moment ago. Right?*

Mitch set his boot down in the shower, turned off the light, and ushered us back to the bedroom where he proceeded to bring me up to speed. The lights were bright and offending as we sat in bed just after 2:00 a.m. I sat cross-legged, facing him as he recounted what happened. I tried to force my brain to catch up and fill in the blanks for me so I could understand from my own point of view, but there was nothing but blackness. The only explanation I could come up with was that I must have blacked out, again.

It was normal for me to get up in the middle of the night to pee. Drinking wine up until the moment you go to bed will do that to you. When Mitch felt me get out of bed that night, he wasn't worried. That is, until he realized I had only walked to the end of the bed and stopped. He opened his eyes to look for me, confused when he saw me at the foot of the bed, slowly lowering myself out of sight for a moment or two. Then, as if all was normal in the world, I stood back up, walked over, and crawled back into bed.

"Where did you go?" he asked, confused.

"To pee," I mumbled as I crawled back under the covers.

He laid next to me in bed, trying to make sense of what he had just seen while I fell back to sleep instantly. He jumped out of bed and turned on the lights. He walked around to the foot of the bed and found a single winter boot standing upright on the floor. When he picked it up, he knew immediately... I had just peed in his boot.

We would later tell the saga over campfires and nights out with friends as some silly story of what a little troublemaker I was for years. "You wanna hear a good story?" Mitch would tease with a wink, and I would turn red as they all looked at me in shock. Laughing, I would add my point of view to proclaim my innocence, stressing the fact that I was sleepwalking and outside of my own control. It was funny, but in a dark, too-close-to-home way.

* * *

I never mentioned to Mitch how much the sleepwalking incident scared me until it happened again. Once, sure, that's a freebie. But twice, that was one frightening step short of becoming a pattern.

I crawled out of bed one morning a few months later and pulled some fresh clothes from my dresser. Mitch looked at me with his head still on the pillow, "Where did you go last night?"

"What do you mean?" I furrowed my brow and tilted my head to the side.

He sat up in bed, grey curls falling over his brow, "You went into the laundry room and closed the door. I guess I didn't think anything of it and fell back to sleep. Then, I woke up to you back in the condo, locking the deadbolt and crawling back into bed."

I stepped away from the door as if it was a trap ready to pull me in. I turned to him, stunned. "What do you mean? I didn't go anywhere. I... Was I sleepwalking again?" I pulled the pile of folded clothes up to my chest, looking down at my hands.

What the hell? How can this be happening?

Standing there dumfounded, I caught the morning light reflecting off the face of my watch. "My watch!" I waved my watch in his direction and ran to grab my phone. It was a GPS watch I wore to track my activities and sleep. "We can look to see if it picked up my movements," I said as I jumped back into bed with Mitch. He scooted over as I opened the app on my phone and began reading him my stats. "I was gone seven minutes, walked 256 steps." I felt like Nancy Drew solving a mystery until the seriousness of it set in.

I had left our home in the middle of the night wearing *nothing* but a rock t-shirt. I walked into the building's community laundry room nearly nude and did who-knows-what for seven minutes. I looked but never found evidence I had even been there. Then, as mysteriously as I had disappeared, I returned, locking the doorknob and the deadbolt before crawling silently back into bed.

Mitch looked at me warily, "That's twice now. Why do you think that's happening?" His curiosity was heartfelt, never one to speak between the lines. Worry started to settle heavily in my chest, disturbed by what it could mean. What might come next.

Sleepwalking was *not* normal. Not for me. *That couldn't be because of alcohol. Could it?* I still thought I was in control of booze, but that narrative was unraveling fast before me. It was one thing to bottle up the hangovers and the constant battle in my head. *That* I could hide. But sleepwalking... suddenly alcohol's effects on me were starting to become visible, leaking through the cracks of my perfect reality. It was no longer a cute little troublemaker tale to laugh at. Like with most sitcoms I grew up with, when you take out the laughter you lose all the brevity and light.

Sometimes reality is a lot darker than we realize, but we can only see it if we're brave enough to look directly at it.

* * *

The next five years passed by the way most do, just a normal life. New careers and pay raises led to a better used car and more bicycles to support our bike racing passion. Mitch and I got into hot yoga and learning to cook occasionally at home. Wedding anniversaries were celebrated with candles and wine, funerals were softened with whiskey. Life kept moving along just as I had hoped, with love, adventure, and companionship.

But somehow, the better my life evolved on the outside, the more intense the war inside of me became. Until it hit me...

You are not going to live to see your fortieth birthday, Kristy.

In the pitch-black auditorium, as the Queens of the Stone Age concert raged on, pieces of the puzzle started to fall into place. The mid-week blackouts, acne that began in my thirties, indigestion and migraines, frequent nausea, and a diminishing appetite. I woke up exhausted every morning and my bones ached in ways I couldn't understand. Anxiety attacks exploded into emotional breakdowns that I would pretend never happened at all. I felt the recognition of each one wash over me in that theater like a side effect reel playing at the end of a prescription drug commercial. An endless list of possibilities I had never thought to watch out for.

The memory of that night haunted my thoughts for weeks after the show. I wasn't sure if alcohol was killing me faster by destroying my body or eroding my will to live. I often drifted off in thought, wondering if there was anything someone could say or do to help me. *What if I was medically ill? Would that be reason enough for me to quit?*

I eventually scheduled an annual check-up with my doctor determined to be honest with someone for the first time about how much I was drinking, a new attempt to get help. Once the day came, the nurse took me back to a room and began walking me through a health questionnaire as the blood pressure cuff tightened around my arm. I tried to breathe slowly as the machine beeped quietly, as if my focus could sway the results. When questions pivoted to alcohol, I mustered up the confidence to answer honestly for the first time in my life.

"How often do you consume alcohol?" she asked.

"Every day," I replied.

"How may drinks would you say you consume on average per day?" she continued.

I took a deep breath. "Five or six glasses of wine. Plus the occasional beers or cocktails on the weekend."

"How many drinks would you say you consume in a given week?" she asked, methodically reading from the list on screen.

I ran the numbers quickly in my head, "Forty to fifty." The rising inflection in my voice made it sound like a question.

After a noticeable pause, she blinked, never looking up from her questionnaire. What I should have said was, "I think I have a problem with alcohol. Every morning I wake up drenched in regret and swear again that it's the last time. But, by the end of the day, I am back to uncorking a bottle and telling myself 'this is our life.' My body feels terrible all the time. My joints, my head, my stomach, my mind, and my heart. But no one else seems to think I have a problem. Am I just no good at handling life?"

Unfortunately, I lost my confidence and let every word die inside me. I sat there hoping somehow she would pick up on the words I left unsaid. If she was at all concerned about the answers I had just given, she gave nothing away until she suggested I take a blood test to check the status of my liver. "Based on some of your answers, we could do a blood test to check your levels." I nodded in agreement, and we continued on with my exam.

I later followed her down the hall to the technician room where the sample would be taken. As the needle pierced my skin, I winced and looked away. I took deep breaths as my face tingled, trying to avoid passing out as my fear of needles sparked panic. My eyes blurred out of focus on a wide-eyed cartoon cat on the wall and that small voice deep inside me whispered, *Maybe bad results would be good for us. It could give us a reason to stop.*

I felt the sting of the needle as the technician pulled it back out of my arm and pressed a cotton ball tight to the tiny hole left behind. I smiled politely but stared down to watch as she finished with a polka dot bandage. "You can wait here for the doctor," she said as she rolled her chair around the corner. I pulled my sleeves down and crossed my arms over my chest, chilled by the thoughts that kept me company.

The doctor returned faster than I anticipated. "Your liver looks good. Nothing to worry about," she said in a clinical, yet encouraging way. I nodded my agreement to her assessment and gathered my belongings. I guess the stigmas that block us from having open, honest conversations about mental health and addiction don't just stop at friends and family. Even the medical team was speechless when I just needed someone to tell me, "Now is an okay time to stop."

* * *

I walked out of the office with less hope than I had walking in. My family and friends never said anything, and now my doctor didn't seem worried either.

Even Mitch didn't seem bothered. After really bad drinking nights when "silly, drunk Kristy" mutated into a raging, fiery bitch who instigated meaningless arguments with Mitch late into the night, I'd wake surprised to find him still sleeping by my side. Incoherent rants and stumbling rampages gave way to painfully bright mornings filled with regret. A few times

Mitch passively tossed out the idea, "Maybe you should cut back" as I laid another desperate apology at his feet.

I would nod along and tell myself, *Sure, yeah, I can do that.* But, deep down, I didn't believe it was true.

People sometimes ask, "Do you know when you became addicted? What happened to cause it?" The genuine curiosity appeals to me. And in the undertones some people hide in their voice, I recognize their own fears peeking out. Holding a mirror up to themselves, looking for some proof that they're not as bad as me. I know because I carried that mirror with me everywhere I went.

It wasn't until I began writing this book that I saw how far my ties to alcohol stretched, how deep the ropes dug into my skin. But coming out of that doctor's office was the first time I ever admitted to myself that I was, in fact, addicted to alcohol.

I am addicted to alcohol. Now where do we go from here?

Eye of the Hurricane

—

moments when
LIFE
feels
OVERWHELMING

we're caught
in a
hurricane

somewhere out on the
ocean
rocked by
waves of emotion

dashed by
demands from
EVERYONE around us

blown about
by the MOODS
and
OPINIONS
of others.

Eye of the Hurricane —me, age 15

* * *

It took two glasses of wine just to feel normal by the time I had reached my mid-thirties. Whether work was stressful or exciting, whether I was sad or just fine, every day ended in wine. I used to think of it as a treat or a special accompaniment to a celebratory meal. It was a social lubricant at book club with the amazing ladies much smarter and more sophisticated than me. But somewhere in between the dinner and book clubs, the indulgent treat turned into a daily habit. It took the edge off after work, paired with the flavors of my meal, and late into the night I would keep pouring until my night cap ran dry.

Each night I would try not to fumble as I made my way to bed, passing out instantly after kissing Mitch goodnight. Every morning, however, began with a storm.

On the weekdays, I would get up and hurry off to work so accustomed to being hungover I no longer realized how crummy I truly felt. With black coffee in hand, I would pick at my microwaved breakfast as I settled into my desk by 7:00 each morning, an hour before my peers would start to arrive. The hum of the office vents and florescent lights overhead became the soundtrack as I sat alone with my thoughts and made out my day's to-do list. With each sip of bitter dark roast that passed my lips, a voice inside would rise and interrupt it all.

A storm of anxiety would build inside my chest, swirling as it rose, taking over my thoughts as they tumbled around inside my head. *How much did I drink last night?* Maybe it was a

Tuesday. Could have been Thursday. I was blacking out in the last few hours almost every night and each morning I woke with the same fear. *How did I get to bed? Oh, shit, think think... Is Mitch mad at me?* I sat there, picking at my travel pancake with a plastic fork as I stared blankly at my emails, tearing through the rubble of my memories from the previous night, piecing together any pictures I could find. I tried to recreate the scene in my mind without anyone knowing I had blacked out again.

I spent the first part of each day raging a war against myself over how much I had drank. *What's wrong with you? Maybe we should stop. It's okay, I'll be better today. I won't even stop at the liquor store on the way home.* Disbelief twisted and intertwined with anger as fear eventually gave way to defeat. *What did I say last night? Did we get in a fight? He's going to leave me... that's what I deserve.*

I sat heavy like a stone in my chair as I held the weight of those thoughts. The massive force of feeling unworthy of my husband's love pressed the air from my lungs. Feeling like my family didn't want me around was a boulder I couldn't move. Every way I doubted myself added to the pile of self-hate that buried me in place.

Hours would pass as the torture continued and spilled into every area of my life. I was the lead inventory analyst on my team and a mentor, yet I would beat myself up over my performance at work, my appearance, over every decision I made in recent days. I felt powerless to the surges of worry and doubt that churned wildly in my mind, all the while a portion of me kept trying to move forward in my day. *Okay, this presentation is ready for next week. I am certain I bombed in the last meeting. Stop that. C'mon, focus! I'll never get that job. I'm stuck here.* Eventually, my coworkers would arrive to start their day, activity building around me as we moved in and out of meetings through our morning. All the while, I tried to hide the storm that raged inside me with a bland smile and determined focus on the work to be done.

By midday, my inner voice would run out of steam and fade into a hush. Like standing inside the eye of a hurricane, it would feel like the winds had calmed and stormy skies parted for sunny blues. The self-doubt and loathing would cease temporarily, and I would pivot full sail into anything that would hold my attention. Meteorologists warn that the eye of the storm isn't as safe as it feels. The rest of the tropical cyclone is never far behind.

A few hours later, as if on cue, the typhoon would build again and it felt like life was closing in on me. Each day, I was tossed around by the wrathful current inside my mind, taking the beating I couldn't control. By the time the afternoon gave way to the evening and more alcohol worked its way out of my system, the anxiety and inner critic would close in on me again and I would collapse under the pressure. *I'm just a drunk, that's all. This is my life... the way it will always be.* I would surrender, plan a liquor store run, then accept my place in life as a drunk once again.

You cannot see the eye of a hurricane while standing outside of the storm with the naked eye. It is only detectable by radar as a convergence of air from every direction is forced into the center by the rising air of the eye wall (WW2010 n.d.). I could feel a pressure building around me, trapped in a vicious assembly of searing emotions inside my own mind. By nightfall with drink in hand, I started to look at my husband as we lounged on the sofa before bed thinking to myself, *Would he miss me if I was gone? Would anyone? Or would they all just go on as if I had never been here?*

The hopelessness twisted with the thoughts in my mind, and I gulped my wine, longing to wash them out to sea along with everything else. Lucky for me, someone in my life had the radar to see the turbulent storm within me before it was too late.

* * *

The year before I quit drinking alcohol for good, I was hanging out with Mitch and a few of our bike teammates after a ride. The sun was high and unseasonably warm that fall afternoon as we congregated, rehydrating with beer and soda as we shared tales of epics rides we'd been on. Before we all parted for the evening, our teammate Donna approached me with a smile on her face. "Hey K, would you like to go to dinner with me sometime?" Donna was an idol of mine long before she knew my name, both as a bike racer and one of the kindest people I had ever met. We were getting closer as friends, but we had never actually hung out just the two of us.

"Of course," I replied with shock and enthusiasm. We traded phone numbers like teens and parted ways after planning a time and place for our dinner rendezvous.

Donna and I met at a hip new diner in Minneapolis. She's twelve years my senior and ages wiser than me. An incredibly intelligent research scientist by trade and National Champion level cyclist for entertainment, I have admired Donna since the day I met her. I had no idea what drove her to invite me out, but she always had the best stories so I knew it would be a good time regardless.

We sat in a booth along the diner window, and I ordered a beer, Donna a shake. She's from the East coast, so there was no passive aggressive delay or beating around the bush with her. Donna came right out and cleared the air of any mystery, "Before we order, I want to tell you why I invited you to dinner. That way we can leave if you don't want to stay."

"Sure, what's up?" my skin tingled with an apprehension, but I trusted her and planted my feet in place.

Donna put her menu down on the Formica tabletop and looked me in the eyes. "I can tell something is wrong. You don't seem happy." I gave her a small smile as some reassurance that I wasn't running out the door just yet. "There is nothing wrong with being depressed," she continued. "I just want you to know you are not alone."

* * *

Growing up in a stoic Midwestern home in the eighties required bottling up emotions indiscriminately. Forced to live in a grey area where celebrating achievements was too boastful and nothing in life was deemed fair. There were usually one or two tears that would sneak out before I could rein in my sorrows and frustrations. Then, I'd take a deep breath and shove them deep inside my emotional vessels and pretend that nothing was wrong. I did everything in my power to be the good little girl I was expected to be.

Whether bottles are made of glass or intestinal fortitude, each one has a breaking point.

When I was young, prolonged periods of stowing away the scorching heat of my rage and arctic loneliness gave way to explosive breakdowns without warning. The bottles I kept fathoms below my surface ruptured, spewing shards of glass across every aspect of my life, invisible cuts bleeding me dry. My dad would lead me into the kitchen, sobbing and breathless, and sit me down in one of the brown vinyl chairs. He would pull a shiny lacquered quote off the wall and ask me to read it out loud.

"Those who bring sunshine into the lives of others cannot keep it from themselves," I would choke out between breaths as I tried to regain control of myself.

"You bring sunshine into my life, baby. Don't keep it from yourself." It was the only conversation we ever had about mental health, but it was one we had often.

I read it each time my school bully teased me because my mom lived somewhere else. "You don't have a family," he'd announce to the other kids in class, laughing and pointing as I tried not to show him my tears.

I sobbed through the words after I threw my model train down the laundry chute, not realizing that dirty clothes and plastic toys didn't land on concrete quite the same.

I read it because of the girls who weren't allowed to attend my slumber parties since there was no woman living in our house.

I clenched my teeth and read it when the other kids called me "spoiled" because I got two Christmases. They didn't know I asked Santa to reunite my parents so I could go back to one.

When I got a bloody nose and detention for standing up for myself on the playground, I read it again.

I read it after I melted my Barbie doll in the clothes dryer, too.

Sitting in the kitchen, I held the wooden plaque in my trembling hands. I traced the images of branches that surrounded the words with pudgy little fingers, hoping to absorb some of its light through my skin. I was desperate to find a way to do as I was told, vehemently hoping to feel the sunshine for myself.

* * *

I remember the day the media announced that comedic genius Robin Williams died by suicide like a marker of time in my life. Listening to the shocked responses of friends, family, and news anchors exposed a new revelation for me. I saw for the first time the vast differences of understanding between those who have experienced depression and those who had not. The solemn responses from those who know the dark abyss of depression intimately were a far cry from the shock felt by those lucky people out there who have never found themselves in that hole.

People passed judgment around like a collections' basket at church, everyone weighing in with their two cents while the depressed ones silently recognized his pain as a reflection of our own. I thought of the quote Dad would make me read when my world shattered outside my control. Williams was a true bringer of sunshine to others. The voices and characters, the wildly honest and energetic standup comedy, the way he stretched out, "Good morning, Vietnam!" Every external portrayal of himself was loved around the world, taking our eyes off his struggles with addiction to alcohol and cocaine. His death saddened me, knowing he must have had those days when he couldn't feel the sun's light for himself.

An author and life coach friend of mine, Natalie, lost her husband to alcohol-related suicide when he was only forty-four years old. "So much of the trauma that my husband experienced was in childhood in such a blind spot he couldn't see it," she said, describing the years leading up to his death. "The mind doesn't know yesterday's pain from today's pain. Pain is pain." Listening to her describe his struggles in his final years felt like a reading from my own internal scrolls.

Links between alcohol addiction and suicide have been found in studies as far back as the 1800s, but the true understanding of how intertwined they really are still intrigues researchers to this day. Scientists reviewed decades of studies on the connection between suicide attempts, ideations, and alcohol abuse from around the world. They found "depression is frequently a precursor of alcohol abuse, but alcoholism may also trigger or exacerbate depression" (Pompili et al 2010). Those of us struggling with alcohol addiction often see drinking as a method for handling inconceivable emotions and psychological stress. But, since alcohol is also a contributing factor to depression, it only exacerbates the problems rather than treat them.

Like pouring gasoline on an already raging fire.

* * *

I stared back across the diner table at Donna, knowing by the soft tone she ended with that she had said all she wanted to say. Life moved on around us like normal, music drifting in from the kitchen as the ring of a bell signaled hot food was ready for delivery. The distant tings of silverware on ceramic plates felt mundane yet comforting as I tried to be confident and strong. I thought my secrets were under control, thought I had everyone's eyes on the version of me I pretended to be.

Sitting there with Donna proved my walls were starting to crumble. My pain was beginning to leak out into the open, exposed for the trained eye to see. I hadn't yet admitted out loud that I was depressed to anyone, not even myself, so I settled on a less vulnerable reply, "We can stay."

We ordered our dinners and started talking the moment our server stepped away. She spoke first, "I can tell you are struggling because I have been there too." Donna opened up about her own battles with depression years prior and the similarities she saw in me. "It's okay to not be okay."

"Oh, yeah," I nodded in agreement with a furrow in my brow, "I know." I said it less because I believed it and more to suggest to myself that I *should* know that. But how do you explain to someone that your abuser is yourself? I couldn't find the words to articulate how the self-hatred was destroying me, tearing me apart one piece at a time. *Why couldn't I just be happy like everyone else?*

Donna interrupted my thoughts with the same precision she wields in the lab. "I also want you to know that you don't have to stay sad forever. There is help out there." She took a sip of her water, and we sat in silence for a moment as I tried to gather my words, any words.

"Thank you. I really appreciate you inviting me here," I used the gratitude to buy myself some time to think up a more thoughtful response. Mental health stigmas were changing by this time in my life, seeing commercials on TV that encouraged people to talk about their feelings and social media pushing ads for therapy. All the while, I was still operating under the stigmas of my childhood. I was struggling to get past the "suck it up" attitude I was raised with and I didn't yet have the skills to ask for help.

This sadness she could see in me was the same that flooded me the night at the concert the year prior. It never left me. Yet here I was, getting closer to forty but my emotional health still hadn't improved. "I *am* depressed. I'm sad all the time.

I don't think I even understand why," it spilled out with the same sting ripping off a bandage leaves behind.

That voice, the one that called me to attention in the darkness of the theater bellowed out from the abyss down inside me... *Or, maybe it's the drinking.* My hands let go of the pint glass of beer I'd been holding for stability, worried the echoing thoughts inside my head would draw attention to the culprit in front of me. My feet fidgeted on the floor like a spout attempting to drain the tension from my body.

Donna never asked why I was sad, simply respected my privacy while trying to ensure I knew I wasn't alone. She shared her experiences with therapy and mental health resources she recommended I look into. We talked for over an hour, pausing to listen to one another and chew. "I feel like such a failure. No matter how hard I try to be happy, deep down inside I'm not." It was as honest and raw as I could handle, teetering on the edge of tears that night. Her sincerity and outpouring of tenderness somehow made it easier to breathe.

The next morning, I searched for my company's employee assistance hotline. With tears streaming from my eyes and a lump in my throat, I dialed the number and broke when the operator asked how she could help. "I am so sad, I think I need help," I said as I placed my hands over my mouth in shame. The woman on the other end of the phone spoke softly and reassuringly as she scheduled an appointment for me with a therapist the following week.

I went to my five free sessions and talked about the overwhelming sadness that plagued me, the anxiety and disabling fear of failure. I thought my screaming inner voice meant that I was broken, that I didn't have it together like everyone else. But I never told the therapist about my drinking. I couldn't bring myself to explore the naming of the beast. Rather, I just kept pointing the finger at myself. I still wasn't ready to admit out loud the power it had over me. And I couldn't yet make the connection that the inner battles were over the drink all along.

Donna was right. It was okay to not be okay. Opening the door for that tough conversation was like a hurricane making landfall. Without the energy of the warm ocean waters feeding into the storm, it weakens and eventually dies off (Hurricane Structure n.d.). Talking about what I was going through felt as though the volatile energy was getting drained from the storm.

There in the diner, with bright lights casting a stark contrast against the cool, dark night outside, I found a small, tiny glimmer of hope.

The Ghost of Christmas Kristy's Past

___

If the inner voice that spoke to me at the Queens of the Stone Age concert was the ghost of Kristy's present, I was about to meet the ghosts of Kristy's past and yet to come. Those bitches made present look like Mother Theresa.

Much like Ebenezer Scrooge in Charles Dickens' *A Christmas Carol*—the three ghosts showing him painful truths about his past, the current suffering of others he had caused, and a frightening future yet to come—I could only hope to wake up a softer, gentler, more caring woman, too. I fondly remember watching the movie every December when I was growing up, intrigued by the haunting experience Scrooge endures and the monumental transformation he makes; as an adult going through these trials, I hoped the same for myself.

* * *

It was a crisp Sunday afternoon in September. Mitch and I were hanging out by a bonfire in jeans and hoodies, awaiting an awards ceremony for the cyclo-cross race we had just finished. Mitch won his race and was waiting for his prize. My battle in the women's race was hard-fought, but I finished just outside of the top three places. The fierce competition left me tired and my muscles sore, so I leaned on cold beers to soothe my aches away while chatting with our friend Gus about bikes and life.

"So, I'm doing 'Sober October' starting tomorrow," Gus stated as he looked down at the koozie-wrapped beer in his hand. The term was new to me but, based on the name, it seemed like a bold move for my reliable drinking buddy.

"What's that?" I asked, genuinely intrigued.

"It's this challenge where you don't drink alcohol for the entire month of October," he explained. "I've been hittin' it hard lately. Thought I'd take a break."

Before giving my mind a moment to organize a protest, I spouted out, "Interesting. I'll do it too." I nodded along with my statement as if I was trying to physically convince myself to go along with the idea. It sounded like the scratch of a record inside my head as the realization of what I had just committed to sank in all the way to the bottom.

"Yeah, you just **don't drink**. Look it up online, you'll find tons about it," Gus finished. I took a large gulp of my pale ale and let the thought of "Sober October" bob and float in the beer a moment or two before I swallowed. We continued to discuss our personal inklings about our own alcohol consumption and follies with the same nonchalance as the weather. As friends came and went by the fire, the conversation shifted into bike race recaps and plans for the week ahead. Once Mitch had his podium presentation, we gathered his prizes and headed home.

For the rest of the afternoon and well into the evening, I thought off and on about not drinking for the entire month of October. *This could be the perfect way to see if alcohol is the root cause of all my distress.* October was always a busy month for us with racing, celebrating our wedding anniversary, and tons of live music. All of them were typical reasons for me to justify drinking to my heart's content. *How's it gonna go if I tell people I'm not drinking? What will they think of me? I guess I'll just figure it out,* I thought to myself. I proceeded to fill my wine glass a few more times before stumbling off to bed around midnight.

* * *

October 1 came with the same slow, fearful awakening as most mornings that had come before it. Before I even opened my eyes, I knew I was already exhausted. Just another shitty night of drunken sleep that left me more tired than rested. I tried to do a quick mental replay of the night to make sure I hadn't started another fight with my husband for no reason. *No, I think we're good,* I thought to myself as I snuck out of bed to get ready for work. "Sober October," I whispered as I put on mascara in the bathroom mirror. I paused a moment to let it settle in after I had finished getting ready then hustled off to work.

I barreled into Sober October like a blind-folded bull, bucking wildly in a rodeo. I had no idea what I was doing or where it would go. Something about this new idea was like the bucking strap tied tightly around the bull's abdomen: I could feel it constricting on me already, irritating and piercing. I couldn't sit still.

Day one was filled with determination and a lot of unanswered questions bouncing around inside my mind. *What do I do on my way home from work if I'm not stopping by the liquor store for more wine? Is there a special trick to this?* Returning home from work that night with only my backpack and a case of sparkling water in hand felt mildly triumphant. I placed the case on top of the minibar in the corner of the living room, having shoved all the remaining bottles of booze to the back of the bottom shelf. *Out of sight, out of mind*, I told myself.

My body pulsed with jittery energy, searching for relief as I paced from room to room. I stepped into our little retro kitchen, taking in the pile of dishes that had sat soiled in the sink for days. Mold started to peek through between the plates on something that once resembled cheese. It was and still is one of my least favorite household chores. As a kid, I would roll my eyes when Dad would say, "We don't need a dishwasher. I have you!" I would not get my first dishwasher until the year I turned forty. Hands down my favorite appliance I ever had.

Once the dishes were washed and stacked in the rack to dry, I began idly tidying up the clothes and mail strewn haphazardly about the condo. Picking up shoes instead of a wine glass, dusting, organizing, my hands and feet refused to rest. Anything to control the fidgeting and keep my mind off the obvious void in my routine. Once I ran out of steam for cleaning, I grabbed my laptop and a can of sparkling water, settling into the corner of our dark brown leather sofa trying to unwind.

"I guess I should find out what this 'Sober October' is about," I told myself out loud as I opened up my laptop to begin my search. I opened one of my favorite social media sites and searched "Sober October." Pages of photographs with people holding framed placards that read "100 days sober," "1,000 days sober," "1 week alcohol-free." Memes and motivational quotes by recovering alcoholics and drug addicts were hard-hitting and honest. Somehow it pushed a small bit of my apprehension to the side. *Maybe this won't be that bad.*

After a couple days sober, my body began to feel physically better. My skin cleared of its blotchy, red patches and took my morning nausea with it. A whole week went by without worrying I had started a pointless argument with Mitch while in the middle of another blackout. Unfortunately, getting through each day wasn't getting much easier. Similar to when the World Health Organization told us to not touch our faces at the beginning of the COVID-19 pandemic: you never realize how much you touch your face until someone tells you not to do it. *What am I supposed to do with my hands? And why can't I stop touching my face?* But with alcohol addiction, it's more like *What am I supposed to do with all this time? And what am I supposed to do with my hands?* I wanted to peel the label or pop the tab off everything I held just to keep my fingers occupied.

By the middle of the second week, I was no longer dizzy in the morning or in the shower when washing my hair. I couldn't remember the last time I closed my eyes in the shower for more than a moment. Now, I could close my eyes and let the hot water wash gently down my face. Breathing shallow so not to suck it into my nose, I imagined the tension washing away down the drain, leaving me peaceful and still.

Even more impactful than the return of my balance was the sudden realization that the screaming voice in my mind had eventually gone quiet. That cruel, unrelenting shrew was now taciturn, observing politely from the sidelines, satiated by my newfound sobriety.

It was actually quite lonely in the silence; somehow I missed the comfort of the abuse. If not for the tightness in my chest that had finally broken free, I might have picked up a glass in that moment. But in the stillness, I could finally take a deep breath all the way down to my toes. What remained in the void was tranquility. I was unsteady but I was beginning to believe I could do this.

What's the old saying...
"Nothing worth it comes easy?"
Or is it, "What comes easy won't last, what lasts won't come easy?"
Either way, I should have known.

A few days later, I was hanging out at the local bike shop my husband worked at, waiting for him to wrap up his day so we could head out for a Friday night bike ride through South Minneapolis. I spoke with two friends of mine, standing in my Lycra cycling apparel and helmet, while they wrapped up their shopping for the day. Unexpectedly, we were interrupted by a man I never saw walk in.

"Kristy. Hi." I blinked at him, curious how he knew my name, unable to place him at all.

"It's me. Jack," he said, flashing a half smile, willing my memory to stir.

It hung in the air as my mind repeated his words back to me like a court stenographer. *It's me. Jack.* There was something familiar in his voice, in the slight lisp in his words.

And in one swift, escaping breath it all came back to me. Who he was.
Then, without warning, who *I was* back then came along with it.

For the first time in more than ten years, ghosts of Jack and my past leapt up out of their box and swirled around me as I stood frozen in place. Jack's disarming smile and the subtle lisp that added enthusiasm to whatever topic he was on. He had come into my life during a time when I was young, aching to figure out who I was. His confidence had attracted me like a moth to a flame back then, hypnotizing and dangerous beyond measure. A season of excess, indulgence, and heartache.

On autopilot, I fumbled out an "Oh, hi." My eyes flickered to my husband and friend Pete checking over our bikes on the sidewalk, oblivious to my discomfort inside. Jack and I exchanged niceties cordially as my trepidation began firing and arching like a live wire. I spoke slowly to avoid a stammer, nodding as he told me about his wife and kids. "That's my husband," I said, gesturing toward the shop's front window.

"I know," he replied, and a shiver ran through me.

Anxiety spun rapidly inside me, a generator of uncontrolled power building energy, spinning faster with each beat of my heart. Pain and anger exploded like chemical reactions, burning me from the inside as I tried to keep it from my face.

"Ready!" Mitch called from the doorway. I excused myself as swiftly as my evening had fractured into dozens of razor-sharp splinters, never looking back.

Mitch, Pete, and I pedaled away from the shop on knob-by-tired bikes so we could take our adventures off the beaten paths that night. We jabbered lightly on our way toward the urban trails by Fort Snelling, hidden, unmaintained trails lined with overgrown grasses and woven with roots atop the damp soil.

Fort Snelling is a military fort built in the 1800s on land that had sacred history, believed to be the site where the Dakota Indian tribe originated. In the US-Dakota war, more than 1,600 Dakota men were imprisoned at the fort, numerous hanged. Fort Snelling, its cemetery on site, and Pike Island are among the most haunted places in Minnesota. People have reported seeing ghosts of men roaming the hallways, strange sounds and smells in the buildings. Gliding apparitions in the distance are rumored to materialize, drifting between the trees in their nocturnal resting place. Men from both sides appearing and vanishing into the shadows of the cemetery. Now, they even offer guided haunted tours.

I should have realized I couldn't run from my ghosts there. Rather, I think the atmosphere called them back.

The discussion dwindled as we lined up single file to enter the trail and I took the caboose position so the two faster men could pedal their own speeds. Low branches slapped me in the face as the loose earth flew up from my wheels. The soft crunching of sticks started as a peaceful relief, a connection with the earth as I tried to separate from the shock of what had just happened.

Crack. Snap. Crunch. We wove through the raw trail around bushes and down steep embankments, clamored over roots and pounced up punchy climbs. I thought I was out-running them. Thought I was getting away.

Snap. Ting. Thud. With each breaking twig and branch, flashes of ghosts appeared in my eyes. Memories flared like scenes from a movie.

Moments in my life I had completely forgotten were clear as day. I tucked them so far at the bottom, I forgot they were there. The emotions and feelings so real in the moment, I had to struggle to focus on the dirt trails that lay in front of me. As I saw myself in Jack's bedroom, drunk again, having answered his 2:00 a.m. call, my chest ached and tightened as the taste of my tears came back to me. I could feel the fracture of the broken heart, the rejection I had felt back then. A younger me had cried and asked, *Why wasn't I good enough for someone nice? Someone who liked me for me.*

Memories twisted around me like ropes, burning into my arms with their course weave. I pedaled harder and kept pace with the men, using my legs to fight as I felt the ropes digging into my flesh. Late night rendezvous, endless pitchers of beer and karaoke at the local dive bar, fake IDs, the DUI, blackouts, and binging. I had repressed it all.

My legs stomped furiously on the pedals, my heart pumping as if preparing for war. The guys spoke off and on, but I stayed silent, focused on the battle within me. With the two of them in front, I could zone out and just do what they do, riding on autopilot with their asses to guide my way.

Flash. *Why were you such an idiot? Why were you such a drunk?* **Snap.** *You were such a mess.* **Crack.**

It was suddenly two ghosts, the memory of three of us in Jack's bed. I had buried it so deep, at first I didn't think it was real.

BOOM!

It was so vivid and realistic, I worried the men could see it too. I dug my heals toward the ground and forced lungs to fill my chest so deep I hunched like a beast. A scowl hardened across my face, and I tried to remind myself they were not real by taking a moment to eat a few energy chews from my pocket. When I drank, I let the water splash from my mouth unabashedly, wearing the dampness like warpaint.

We returned to the shop, sweaty and dirty from the intense effort. Pete pulled up next to me on the sidewalk, enthused with the energy on the ride, "You were flying tonight!"

"Just had a fire, I guess," I said as I shrugged off the confirmation of what remained surging through me. It was as if someone had torn through the stitches of a wound I never healed. Releasing the ghost of who I was back then, now staring me square in the face.

For the next few days, the ghosts snuck in and surprised me unexpectedly. It was futile as I tried to distract myself with cooking, cleaning, scorching hot showers, and blaring music loudly in my headphones. Riding my bike, there was a layer of anger mixed into my effort each night and I was twisted inside about how the fury was making me faster.

I struggled with myself, wrestling with questions I hadn't thought of in years. *Why was he such an asshole? Why did he treat me that way?* I was too afraid to tell Mitch any part of the memories that chased me through each day, too afraid it would be the final straw to drive him away. I silently suffered, unsure of what the old memories resurfacing meant. Too ashamed to look back at that time in my life.

By day twenty-one, the blind bull approach to staying sober failed, and I fell off the wagon at our annual Halloween beers-and-bikes cruise with friends. Between the cravings and the ghosts that howled out my transgressions, I was out of coping mechanisms. The day that started with a can-do attitude morphed into me chewing all my nails down anxiously before lunchtime, while I failed terribly at not obsessing about alcohol. By evening, I was chugging a six pack of IPAs to catch up to my friends. Later that night, after I convinced Mitch to stop at the liquor store so I could grab a box of wine, the ghosts finally disappeared.

This time when the ghosts whispered to me about the memories I'd locked away, I had an escape. I had my drink back. Chasing them away just far enough that I could fall asleep fitfully, not knowing any other way.

The Ghost of Kristy's Yet to Come

———

You're a drunk.
This is your life. Deal with it.
This is how it will always be.
Do you think everyone knows? Can they see how deep you
have fallen?
Your best friends wouldn't miss you.
Mitch is better off without you.
It's just a matter of time until you lose it all.

Within a few days of relapsing, I was back to drinking six or more glasses of wine each night, as normal a routine as feeding the dog or kissing my husband good night. My inner voice didn't waste any time putting me back in my place.

I returned to spending the first few hours of every work-day answering emails and fighting with the anguish inside. Before my latest attempt at sobriety, she was frustrated and mean. Now, having glimpsed the mystical oasis up close, she was cruel and angry, screeching louder and longer throughout my day. Disappointed in another failed attempt, gnashing teeth and drawing blood.

What the hell is wrong with you?

I busted my ass and fought my way through anxiety and uncertainty each day, returning to booze each evening as the sun set into the horizon, pulling my willpower down with it into the darkness of night.

Staring into the burgundy elixir that swished in the glass, I began reflecting on the twenty brief days I recently spent sober. I was so focused on the goal then, so determined not to open a beer or tip back another vessel of vino that I hadn't celebrated the milestones along the way. I had craved breakfast for the first time in years after only five days booze-free. The night sweats never worried me until I got sober and noticed they were gone. But they came back in a rush, leaving me drenched each morning, sheets stuck in the creases behind my knees and lines plastered across my skin. That tarnished feeling tunneled down to the core of me.

All the magic of those days were gone, replaced with the same ugly stains and emotional black eyes I was used to. The last week of October bled into November, ushering in the beginning of winter. The shorter days mirrored the dwindling light I felt inside, dragging back with them the blackouts, a level darker than ever before.

I woke suddenly, wrapped in darkness in the still of the night. I scanned the room, lit only by an LED clock along the far wall of the living room. With blurred eyes, I could make out it was after 3:00 a.m. An old comforter warmed me as I looked about the space, perfectly covering me as if I had been tucked in on the couch. I pulled myself up and swung my bare feet to the cold wood floor, rising quietly before tiptoeing to the bedroom.

I could hear Mitch's soft breathing as I neared the curtain that separated our bedroom from the rest of the condo. Quiet puffs of air escaped his lips as he exhaled in the darkness. I crept silently across the soft carpet, climbing into bed as I held my breath in vain, hoping he wouldn't notice. Shame spread through my body as I snuck my feet and legs under the covers, praying I wouldn't wake the dog. He hadn't rustled by the time I laid my head on the pillow. My body was rigid as I curled my knees up to my chest, trying to push away the worry so I could fall back to sleep.

As I made coffee in the kitchen the next morning, Mitch walked in to pour himself a glass of juice. "I couldn't wake you up to go to bed," Mitch said with a sideways glance directed my way. "I tried, but you wouldn't even open your eyes. So, I covered you up and just left you there." I knew it meant I wasn't just sleeping. I was passed out drunk. On a work night. Again. The next few times I woke up alone in the living room, I tried harder to sneak into bed unnoticed. I fell asleep as I breathed shallowly, too afraid to wake him and face up to what I did yet again.

* * *

The Ghost of Christmas Yet to Come in Dickens' *A Christmas Carol* was a mysteriously dark and ominous figure. It appears to Scrooge at midnight, the "witching hour," believed in folklore to be the time when spirits and demons are at their most powerful. It was a large being, cloaked in black cloths that dragged along the ground as it eerily floated toward the frightened man in his bed. Reminiscent of the Grim Reaper, the spirit takes Scrooge to see his own grave, raising a skeleton hand to point at the name etched on the tombstone.

Scrooge pleaded, desperately negotiating for a future other than the tragic one he was being shown: a certain death mourned by no one at all. It was a stark and dire warning before him as he trembled on hands and knees in his sodden nightshirt, the silence between them holding more weight than any words could manifest.

Scrooge awoke suddenly, his hands clutching the curtains the same way he grasped at the bottom edge of the spirit's cloak in the dream, still beseeching the phantom for redemption straight into morning.

Maybe that's the true definition of rock bottom. Whether it be the Grim Reaper or the Ghost of Christmas Yet to Come, it's a necessary experience. That pivotal moment revealing to you a truth you cannot deny, exposing the purest reason at the core of your being that can fill you with enough desire to stop your destructive behavior. That secret place inside you likely forgot was even there.

* * *

Awakening in the darkness of my living room became my personal cemetery ripped straight from Dickens' tale. Moving through the late-night hours, fractured pieces of my heart allowed hopeless sighs to echo out into my world. Dread overtook me. I was disappointed in myself for falling back into the same rhythm that slowly marched me closer to my grave.

But those twenty days sober opened a new door to my heart that couldn't be closed again. Where light trickled in, so did a fledging belief that there was more to life than misery. A small budding of hope. A vision not of the life I wanted to live, I already had that. Illuminated in the most sacred recesses inside me she stood, the image of *who* I always wanted to be.

How could I ever find out if I could be that person if I was never brave enough to try?

A few weeks after Sober October, I stopped searching for reasons to quit and started devouring new ways to quit instead. I had quit cold-turkey freshman year of college with no safety net and found the rejection more than I could bear. Surviving three years sober for someone else in my early twenties was a muted existence I followed while I watched the world spin by from backstage. My recent twenty-day experiment was a powder keg waiting to ignite. Filled with the fiery emotions, self-hate and suicidal ideations, the only outcome was near total annihilation. Now I was determined to try anything, searching for an escape from the life I didn't want to die living.

One evening after work, I sipped my wine while taking in another disgusting pile of dishes in the sink. I decided to begin filling the hours before Mitch got home with researching alcohol, addiction, and recovery to fill the time; things I could listen to while I picked up piles of neglected mess. A few search results online pointed me toward a podcast by Annie Grace called *This Naked Mind*. The description fed the longing in me like nectar, "empowering anyone to question their drinking without fear of labels, stigma, or judgment" (Grace 2017). Within fifty-eight seconds of clicking play, my jaw dropped open as my eyes darted to the laptop screen. I ignored the dishes another moment as I cranked up the volume to full blast.

Annie was telling a story of waking in the middle of the night drunk, immediately filled with regret and dread. The familiar emotions spilled out in her story, ripped from the headlines of my own volatile experiences. "I just start in on myself," she confessed. "Annie, what is your problem? Why can't you get this under control?" the words knocked the wind out of me, my jaw practically breaking at the speed of which it fell. Tears burst from my eyes, and I choked on a sob, *That's just like me.*

I paused the recording a moment to collect myself, looking around the room as if I needed something to hold onto. Spotting the minibar near the kitchen, I grabbed the laptop and shoved a box of wine aside, placing the computer so I could listen to the rest as I scrubbed at the soiled plates. I started the episode from the beginning and filled the sink with hot water and suds. I hung on every one of Grace's words as I washed the dishes on autopilot. For the first time, I was unbothered by the tedium of fighting the dried foods.

By episode two, I was listening via headphones and my cellphone so I could more easily roam from room to room, drinking in her research between long swallows of red wine. Her approach was to inform the curious rather than guilt people for being active drinkers. That declaration somehow made me feel more accepted in the privacy of my own empty home. Mitch returned that evening to find me with an added pep in my step, a secret weapon I believed in yet wasn't ready to reveal.

I found countless recovery podcasts to listen to while at work the next day, analyzing inventory levels of women's pants across the country with headphones on my ears. I took notes of tips for staying sober at concerts and navigating the awkwardness of sober date nights while tracking shipping containers crossing the ocean from Vietnam. I picked up her book of the same title on my way home from work and had dog-eared countless pages by the time I got ready for bed.

I started to tell Mitch what I was doing, how I was thinking of quitting once and for all. Grace's book cited boundless research on alcohol's effects on the mind and body that she had found during her own journey into sobriety. She laid it out as an inform, the most comprehensive education I ever had on such an impactful portion of my life.

"Maybe you could try to not drink so much," he offered tenderly as he pulled the covers back and crawled into bed.

"I don't think I can," I answered, the honesty of it stopping me as I searched his eyes, suddenly afraid of his reply.

"Whatever you think is best," he leaned over and gave me a gentle kiss. He smiled encouragingly and said goodnight. I drifted off, surprised when I counted in my head only three glasses of wine consumed that night.

* * *

I spent hours binging podcasts while I worked and in the quiet hours when I got home, awaiting Mitch to return from his day at the bike shop. I listened to stories shared of experiences like mine, some easier, and some almost too terrifying to believe. It fueled my love of knowledge, continuously searching for more, filling my mind with facts and science, soothing my heart with encouraging light.

In scattered episodes across many different hosts, I heard people mention a recovery method of "playing the tape forward" or "playing the tape through." Employed to prevent relapse, this technique is used by addicts to consider all the outcomes if they give in to their cravings. Beyond the relief. After the regret. *Play the tape forward... What happens next?*

When I was nineteen, I had started having massive panic attacks and bouts of suicidal ideation. Months of bottling my emotions would erupt unexpectedly, my mind racing about everything I needed to do but didn't have time for. Things I needed to accomplish, regrets over things I had said, afraid of things to come. My fears spiraled through my imagination, creating stories about everything in my life that could go wrong. I had a therapist for a year or two who named them my "worry spirals" and challenged me to call them for what they were and move past them. I could back then, with a little help from her prescription pad.

The more I learned about the "play the tape" technique, the more I realized I could put my mental defect to good use.

* * *

For the first time in my life, I took a second look on what alcohol was doing to my body and mind. How prolonged abuse can alter the brain chemistry and emotions. How it fuels depression and anxiety by creating dissonance in mind. How tolerance feeds into cravings and a habit can become an engulfing addiction.

All the while, still drinking my wine and beer each night.

I knew the place alcohol filled in society by now. Booze and spirits were ingrained in every ritual and experience in my life. College. My wedding day. Seeking solace after funerals. Amplifying gatherings with sugary cocktails. From celebrating promotions to venting about my bitchy, micromanaging boss, it was everywhere I turned. As the knowledge grew into discernment, I started to question whether all the social aspects were reason enough to keep drinking. Whether or not the battering of my mental health was worth it just so I could be like everyone else.

The glasses of wine were no longer a casual way to unwind at the end of the day. Not a reliable antidepressant or a harmless celebratory lift. It was the undeniable anchor that kept pulling me down, holding me in place. I was frozen in fear with the last ounce of hope shriveling in my beaten palm.

At once, it was no longer *just* alcohol to me. I started to see for what it was, what life it drained from me, and how I was going to have to face it once and for all.

Thanksgiving came in a blink of an eye, and we found ourselves sitting around my dad and stepmom's dinner table for another holiday meal. The leftovers were already cooling in the fridge and pie thoroughly devoured by the time we opened the eighth bottle of red wine. There were only three of us with wine glasses to fill. I leaned my head on the back of the tall wooden dining chair, holding the stem of the glass between my thumb and forefinger, watching as the liquid splashed up the sides of my glass as my stepsister poured me another round.

In a blink of time, a ripple shrouded in darkness, I woke in my bed at home. I blinked my eyes and stared up at the sparkles on the ceiling as they twinkled in the midmorning light. I dressed and walked into the kitchen and found Mitch pulling the eggs out of the refrigerator. "You girls were *wasted* last night," he said with a snort and eyes wide with disbelief. "I'm glad Melissa let us drive her home."

"We drove her home?" I asked, bewildered. *We drove my step-sister to her place?*

"Yes, we drove her home because you two were trashed." I buried my face in my hands and tried to force my mind to show me what happened, but there was nothing there. I was blackout drunk with my family. *What if that was the last time they saw me? What if that would be their last memory of me? Or my last memory of any of them?* Whispers at funerals flooded back to me.

"You don't remember that?" he asked, genuinely surprised.

"I don't remember ever leaving their house."

I saw it so clear in that moment... I could play the tape forward; I knew this was going to keep happening. Blackouts repeating throughout my life like a Groundhog's Day I would never escape alive. I could see the fissures form between Mitch and me and assume the increasing suffering: Violent combustion of emotions I feared too much to face. Broken hearts and rotting flesh, unhealed wounds still poisoning me, rotting from the inside out.

I let that tape roll through over and over until it frayed at the edges, and I had memorized every possible moment of anguish and heartache that could play out if I kept drinking. I internalized the agony, shoved my hands deep into the battered cavern of my heart and held as its rhythm sputtered and eventually ceased.

* * *

I bounced against disparate levels of rock bottom repeatedly throughout life. Sometimes the fall wasn't too far from the previous height. Other times, I was so fucked up that I didn't even realize I had hit a new low. But something about Thanksgiving was different. For the next two days, I noticed every sip of wine I drank made me feel worse. Every swallow failed to deliver the relief I expected. Gone was the giddy tingle of a buzz of the first drink. The second ushered in sadness. And the next few failed at driving it away.

Both nights, as I tried to drift off to sleep, I saw a vision so vivid it was as if I could reach out and touch it with my unsteady hands.

Alone, I stood in a dark, narrow space. Rough dirt walls with stones and exposed roots were on every side. The opening was mere inches above my head as I took in the earthen hole I stood in, nothing but a full glass of wine in my hand. As I tipped my head back to drink it in, the glass of wine transmuted into a shovel, and I saw my life over the years come through in images. But this time, every time I tipped back a glass in celebration or stress, in grief or in joy, I was actually picking up a shovel full of dirt and tossing out of the opening above.

I saw myself slowly digging myself deeper into the hole. One that grew darker with every passing moment, but I was too busy refilling the glass to notice the change in scenery. The flowers, trees, and sunsets that brought me joy disappeared, replaced by dirt walls, torn roots, and dark eyes reflecting the last of the light that still trickled down from above.

As the well sunk deeper into the earth, my loneliness howled along with the company of the ghosts that still haunted me. I was stagnant, unable to explore or move forward in my life. There were no goals to chase. No sun to bask in. Just the blackness that enveloped every piece of me. Still refilling the glass, still denying the truth.

No, this isn't a shovel. It can't be.

To my surprise, there was no jagged, rocky dirt floor beneath me. Only a clear, glass floor separated me from an endless cavern below.

The years of my life passed by in silence, a regretful blur of memories as I kept digging, always watching the abyss below me with hesitation. Images began to manifest and morph before me in a haze, seeming to grow closer with every passing moment. Over and over, without respite, until I looked down at my raw, torn-up hands and saw the shovel for what it was.

I didn't need to wait until I hit rock bottom to know how far I had fallen... If only I opened my eyes, I would have known the bottom was always in sight.

The silence was eerie as I stared through the glass floor at the nothingness. Flashes of ghosts far below spun wildly in the void, wrapped around skeletons of the dreams and desires I'd once had and allowed to die. Where Scrooge dealt with his discomfort and loneliness by hoarding money, by guzzling gold, I was using the glass to dig my own grave. Where he found immediate relief by bursting into Christmas morning a changed man, I first needed to climb back out of my tomb.

I needed to crawl back into the light, no matter how broken I felt.

* * *

November 30, 2019, just forty-eight hours after Thanksgiving dinner, became my last night of drinking alcohol. I poured myself four or five glasses of wine that evening, finishing off the last box we had. The wooden top to the minibar was stained from years of red wine drips that happened late into the night that I no longer cared to wipe up. I pressed the button to fill my well-abused wine glass, broke down the box, and squeezed the last drops from the bag.

As I sipped slowly on that last glass of merlot, I sat and took full inventory of all the emotions and thoughts that swirled through my mind.

Gabor Maté explained it eloquently in an interview with Brian Rose on *London Real*, "Addiction is not a choice that anybody makes. It's not a moral failure. It's not an ethical lapse. It's not a weakness of character. It's not a failure of will such as our society believes it to be… nor is it an inherited brain disease the way our medical systems often say it is. It's a response to human suffering" (Rose 2019). We as addicts, be it work, drugs, or alcohol, are in a constant state of retreat, using our magic elixir to escape the frightening terrain of our own minds. We often flee from being alone with ourselves and the uncontrolled landscape of our emotions.

I never understood something so simply as I did when I heard that interview for the first time. As I started to peel back the layers to find those same truths in my own lived experience, I started to understand myself at a level I had never known before.

The anxiety, self-doubt, and anger were gaping holes in my heart. The insecurities, fear and lack of self-worth, and jealousy overwhelm huge crevasses that harbored the nothingness inside. I used alcohol to fill them all, to repair them like putty, but it ate away the softest parts of me. It eroded each raw edge like acid, widening every cavity, allowing parts of my true self to seep out and disappear.

All I had ever wanted was to belong. To be cared for, to be missed, to be loved. More than anything, I just wanted to feel whole. *What if I just focus on being me? Who I am without trying to fit into all the boxes of expectations I dance between? What if I could just BE?*

I was addicted to an addictive substance. Simple as that. Now, it was time to try something else.

Now it was time to choose me.

Don't Just Rise...

———

Around the time Mitch and I got engaged, I started a blog about all the adventures we went on, from road trips to bike races, epic concerts to simple surprises found in everyday life. I have wanted to be a writer since third grade but talked myself out of pursuing it when I thought corporate jobs would give me more security and stability than I understood writing to do. My blog was my literary escape, a place where I felt safe to share my thoughts and travel experiences, a replacement for the words I couldn't part my lips for. A small expression of my undying belief I could manufacture a life of my dreams.

I had a decent following for the first five years, occasionally getting recognized by strangers at mountain bike races in the Midwest or social gatherings around the cities. As my addiction to alcohol rooted deeper within me, depression flared and scorched the things that used to bring me joy. I stopped going to book club and quit reading altogether. I lost interest in getting out on Friday nights and secretly celebrated every time a cancellation turned into sweatpants and low lighting at home. Every time I sat down at my laptop to blog about our latest trip, I stared blankly as my self-doubts talked me out of writing once again. *I'm not good enough, this is crap. No one cares.* Eventually, I quit altogether.

One after another, the embers of my dreams flickered and faded, reduced to ash in a pile of who I wished I could be. I had believed people became addicted to alcohol and drugs because they had lost everything. I never realized it was the other way around.

* * *

I laid in bed and blinked my eyes open, listening to the slumbering breath of Mitch and our dog next to me as I took in the soft morning light. A quiet Sunday in December, no alarm set, no obligation forcing me to rise any earlier than my body desired. It was my last "day one."

I bathed in how amazing the feeling of waking up without a hangover was, noticing a new stillness deep down inside. Unlike almost every morning that had come before, there was nothing to hear but three souls breathing softly as the heat drifted out of the vents overhead.

I remained under the heavy black comforter, searching inward for that voice who loudly bayed every time I woke up with another hangover. The voice that had berated and boxed me for years now left me strangely feeling abandoned and alone. The silence was both odd and peaceful, wrapped in a convoluted mass of emotions I tried to name as they tumbled inside my mind. There she sat, deep down inside that little cave at the core of me, with a tiny smile and nod. *We've got this,* was all she said.

This time, I finally believed her.

I spent my entire adult life and some of my youth collecting reasons to quit drinking while only focusing on the discomfort I tried to drink away. Decades of disappointing myself. But as I learned how to change my relationship with alcohol and to evaluate my beliefs around its value, I finally had enough fodder to ignite my personal revolution.

I rolled out of bed, threw on old, cozy sweats and a sweatshirt, then snuck off to boil water for coffee. As it heated, I opened the living room blinds for the first time in years, letting the dust float and dance in the warm light that snuck in the window like bands of gold.

Once the water boiled, I filled the coffee press slowly, observing the grounds as they tumbled in the steaming water. I grabbed the press and a mug from the kitchen, heading to the couch to plop down in my favorite spot. I wrapped a quilt around my legs and opened my journal, focusing on gratitude to jump start the new day. As they came to me, I honored my blessings, big and small.

I am sober.
I am capable of doing anything I set my mind to.
I am grateful for my supportive husband.
Hot, fresh brewed coffee.
No plans for my day.

I sipped my coffee as I tried to dream up ten goals I wanted to achieve in the next ten years. *I am sober* were the first words I wrote down. The rest of my life vision spilled out with sincerity but none of them held the same weight and impact as the first.

My gratitude and my goal wrapped in one tiny, simple sentence: *I am sober.*

I basked in the comfort the declaration instilled in me. Mitch and our dog, Rosco, bounded out of the bedroom an hour later as my stomach growled, and the coffee ran low. I looked him in the eyes and smiled, enjoying the sleepy grin he gave me in return. "Good morning," he crooned in a raspy voice.

"Hi, baby," I replied, peacefully reveling in knowing I had nothing to fear, having remembered every moment of my last day drinking. I tried to think of how to tell him of the plan I was set to unfold as we made breakfast and planned out our day: a load of laundry, a bicycle ride in the cool winter air, dinner together at home. It was a pleasant day filled with activities to keep my mind occupied and hands busy, just in case.

Each time I tried to get sober before ended in failure. Whether I tried to go it alone or use brute force to power through. I crashed and burned through the years, but this time was different. I had broken myself down to such a desperate state that I longed for it to end. I made the choice to not let it kill me. It was up to me now to learn how to live.

There was a little more pleasure in my scrambled eggs and toast that morning, more sparkling of the snow in the high noon sunlight. Even our midday nap felt somehow more relaxing than ever before. At dinner time, I poured a can of chilled Fresca into a fancy glass and held it out for Mitch to see.

"I haven't had a drink all day. I'm done. Today will be my last 'day one.'" I shared my plan to quit drinking indefinitely and how I was still figuring it all out as I went. He was impressed by the sudden change and raised his own glass of soda to me in celebration, sealing the plan with a clink of our glasses.

We lounged on the couch together for the rest of the evening as I shared with him all the research I had found: altered brain chemistry and diminishing memory, fuel for my anxiety, poison to my organs and self-worth. Mitch helped me plan rewards for myself each week as I set out to stay alcohol-free. I shared with him the tips and strategies I collected to make it through each day. By bedtime, we pitched the nine-bottle wine rack to the alley, knowing someone would find it a home, and stashed the wine glasses in the back of the cupboard.

The next morning at work, I sat down and took in the sight of my desk. Everything was as I had left it on Friday, but it felt different. Because I was different. I sipped on a coffee I grabbed from the office café and spied the free letter board they gave us the previous week. Shoved off to the side of my desk, discarded, I reached over and pulled it close. I poured the little, light blue letters onto my desk and laid the green colored board alongside them. *What should it say?* Alone on the fifth floor of our office I pondered, allowing my uncluttered mind to wander through the poems and quotes I think about often. *A line from my favorite poem? A lyric? A quote. But by who?*

Then it hit me. It wasn't a quote I knew from a poster or song, a poem, or a celebrity. That little voice inside cleared her throat and said confidently...

Don't just rise,
SHINE!

The vision of a glorious phoenix rising filled me, brilliant flames reaching to the sky. Fiery reds and oranges danced all around, the mythical beast emerging, reincarnating from its own ashes. Radiating the intense heat of its power, it shaped the air with the strength of its blazing wings.

Destroyed yet destined to live again.

I found each of the letters and placed the tabs into the board to hold them in place then pinned it to the wall of my cube. Soon after, my team started filtering in, gabbing lightly about the weekend and plans for the day. Alexis was the first to notice the sign as she took off her coat in her adjoining cube, "'Don't just rise, shine!' What's that from?"

I shrugged awkwardly and smirked back, "I just thought of it this morning."

"I love it," she exclaimed with her mega-watt smile and bold red lips.

It dawned on me then that Alexis had never seen me drunk, not once. We have laughed together and comforted each other weekly as we tackled the corporate retail landscape, yet I never felt pressured to drink to win her friendship or kindness. *Why should I worry that my family and closest friends will turn on me for choosing to quit drinking?* I knew it was because there was a time in my life that I was rejected for giving up alcohol, but it was time to test the waters again. I straightened up in my chair and looked at Alexis, "I gave up drinking. Today is day two for me."

With more enthusiasm and palpable sincerity, she lit up and pulled her chair closer, "That's amazing! How do you feel?"

Inside my head, I was vomiting out words faster than I could process them: *relieved, scared, happy, good, weird, I really don't know.* I smiled back a real, genuine, stretched-out-to-my-eyes grin and tried to be succinct, "It feels right." Alexis and I spent another few minutes talking about how good it felt to make the decision and take the leap, how easy it was to wake up that morning, how much longer a sober day felt, and the tranquility inside.

The first few weeks were quiet and peaceful without the swarm of regrets creating a ruckus of my thoughts, splitting my focus, and detracting from my tasks each day. In the hush, days became exponentially longer, and the clarity allowed me to concentrate on each moment in time. When thoughts bubbled up about trips to the liquor store, I answered in hopeful confidence, *No, we don't do that any longer.*

For a few hours each night before Mitch returned home, I continued my pursuit of knowledge with more books and podcasts about alcohol and addiction. I used the science of alcohol's impact on the brain, hormones, and mental health to focus on any time a craving arose. I used them to analyze and challenge my own beliefs about the importance of alcohol in my life, keeping my eyes on all the ways I had suffered to make it through each passing day. I reminded myself of how I no longer wished to feel.

The more I understood about what had been going on in my body, the more side effects I recognized for the very first time. I spent each morning reflecting on all the ways my physical and mental health changed as it receded from my body and the focal point of my mind. Gone was the dread, the shame, and self-hate. My red puffy cheeks were now soft and clear. My eyes were less cloudy each day.

As my body healed, so did my confidence.

As I told more friends about the choice I made, they responded with the same excitement and support as Mitch and Alexis, releasing more of my fears into the ether, freeing me from their painful grasp. I was getting sober without avoiding everyone I knew, without shutting myself in or removing myself from the world. I was surviving and determined to pave my way to a life free of addiction.

During the World Series in 1932, legend has it that Babe Ruth called a home run after two strikes by extending his arm out long and pointing out at center field as if to say, "I'm sending this one over the wall." On the next pitch, Babe sent the baseball over the center field fence for a home run. While some say he was annoyedly responding to the heckling from the opposing team's bench, Babe himself admits to calling his shot. According to the National Baseball Hall of Fame, "people still argue whether he was pointing or not. It will always remain in baseball folklore" (Horne n.d.).

I believe if Babe says he called his shot, then it's exactly what he did. Now it was my turn. I was going to call my shot. Like Babe Ruth, I pointed at center field and told the world around me I was gonna knock this one out of the park.

After a few, long and steady weeks sober, I sat down at my laptop determined to dust off my old blog and write again. I knew the best start would be the opening chapter into a whole new life, a new beginning into the unknown. Still jabbed by a tinge of doubt that urged me to stop, reminding me I gave up writing long ago, I trudged forward anyway. My fingers tapped at the keys as my thoughts came to life, dancing methodically as I slowed for the intensifying emotions. I shook off the fear of my past to embrace the power of who I was setting out to become, looking out into the world to discover who was coming with me.

I shared the post on social media and muted all notifications for twenty-four hours, instantly petrified of what was going to happen next. There was no turning back now.

I mustered up the courage to check for comments early the next day, excited energy coursing through me as I logged into the site. The post received more support and comments than I ever anticipated. Friends I didn't even know were sober anonymously reached out to me in private messages, texts, and voicemails. Comments bursting with encouragement and love tightened my throat as tears pricked my eyes.

A handful of people contacted me for advice on their own questions about their relationship with alcohol, asking for more details around how I made the change. As the days turned into weeks, every conversation I had about what I was going through made the fear of this new sober life dissolve away a little more. I was open about whether it was a good day or a bad day, what my worst day drinking had ever looked like. The more I stood in the light about my experience, the more people stepped up to stand alongside me.

As I spoke out loud about what I had been going through and what I set out to find in a sober life, the stronger I became. The better I felt. The less I wanted to drink.

Pretending to have my life and my insecurities under control was exhausting. I played a character for nearly my entire existence. Stashing my depression and struggles behind brick walls inside my mind wasn't working. Keeping it all a secret had been killing me. Recovering out loud? That was the key to finding out who truly had my back. A stage for me to announce who I now was. No longer "Boozie the Clown," no hiding in shadows, quivering lips trapping my cries for help. I was just Kristy, wiping away the blackened seer to let a little light shine through.

My friend Dani once told me about her first year sober, "I spent so much time not knowing who I was." Her sentiment was so accurate and all-encompassing, reassuring to know I wasn't alone. I had ditched all my safety nets, my comforts and routines, to test the hardest theory I have ever faced. I might not have yet truly known who I was, but I knew who I no longer wanted to be.

I called my shot that I was sober and set the bar to dictate how my future interactions would go. Rather than being shy and passive with my reasons, I took a firm stance to showcase my resolve. Displaying the value in the choice I was making eliminated room for people to object. By admitting my weakness, my struggles, I slammed the door on people who might suggest I didn't have a problem from their point of view. I was tired of waiting for everyone's approval of my decision, waiting for everyone else to give me permission to reclaim my life. *This is me; take it or leave it. Just don't be an asshole while you're here.*

I approached every situation as a new experience and tried to be prepared for everything. I went to friends' homes with nonalcoholic beverages stashed away in my purse. I packed a cooler full of sodas and seltzers to enjoy after mountain bike rides with our teammates and friends. For social events and larger gatherings, I worried the social norms of drinking were going to drive more resistance or pushback. To be prepared, I built a library of answers in my mind for the questions I anticipated would come. *Can I get you a drink? No, why not?* In all honesty, it's never anyone's business, but you can never be too prepared.

While my supporters accepted me the moment I told them I quit drinking, the rest of the world still approached me from a place of social customs and expectations. Lucky for me, being from Minnesota became my super power, giving me the ultimate advantage to turning offers down.

In Minnesota, it's customary to reject all offers twice, only accepting on what is known as the "third offer." Author and radio personality Howard Mohr explained that "abrupt and eager acceptance of any offer is a common mistake made by Minnesota's visitors." Instead, it is customary to only accept on the third offer, and to do so with a tone to indicate you accept but vehemently against your best interests (Mohr 1987). The common exchange of declinations that eventually flip to acceptance made the topic of consent a murky conversation in my formative years. But now, knowing how to say "no" repeatedly was just plain fun.

Allow me to explain... If a Minnesotan host asks, "Would you like a cookie?" a visitor should never reply with "Yes, I'd love one. What flavors do you have?" The brazen acceptance would throw off the entire exchange and leave your kind-hearted host speechless. Instead, a more traditional banter would proceed in a cadence similar to this:

"Come on in! Would you like a cookie?" asks the Minneso-tan host.

"No, thank you," the visitor says politely.

"Really, it's no trouble. I just pulled them out of the oven."

"That's okay. I wouldn't want to put you out."

"I've got some on a tray all nice and cool for you to enjoy."

Visitor, finally conceding: "Yeah, sure. I guess I can have one."

"How about some coffee to go with that?"

"No, this is great. No need to make coffee." A second cycle through the "third offer" begins.

As Mitch and I ventured out to parties and concerts, I started out simple with replies such as, "I just quit drinking."

"I am sober cab tonight."

"Nope, thanks, I'm good with Fresca."

The less close the friendship of the people we were with, the more confused they were when I wouldn't accept once the third offer was given. It was like I disrupted all they knew, forcing them to keep asking. I took that as an opportunity to get a little more mischievous with my responses hoping to end the cycle.

"Ope, no thanks. Beer gives me the shits."
Whispering uncomfortably close, "Wine makes my ass itch."
"I shouldn't, it's a term of my parole."
"You don't want to see me when I'm blacked out. Seriously... it's so bad, *I* don't even remember."

Bold, culture-bending responses like these came in handy with the really drunk folks, with the people who weren't actually listening. Dropping them with an impish smirk on my face, I almost drooled waiting for their reply.

Mitch and I met a bunch of friends to see The Cult in concert at the Palace Theatre in St. Paul, MN. While we were hanging out between bands, an acquaintance named Ben threw his arms around Mitch and my shoulders, grinning widely. "Hey, how's it going? Can I get you a drink? Anything you want!" He was gregarious, loud, and obviously intoxicated before the concert even began. He slurred slightly, his friendly Minnesotan offer laid out for us.

"I'm good," Mitch responded as he lifted the clear plastic cup of cola in his hand.

"We're good," I reinforced with a nod toward my empty glass.

"No really, what can I get you? My treat!" Ben insisted.

Bucking the third offer rules, I accepted on the second, "I'll take a Sprite, then. Thanks!"

"Sprite? No, you can have WHAT. EVER. YOU. WANT." He swayed as he enunciated each word.

Smiling playfully, I leaned into the imaginary game he didn't know we were playing, "Sprite. I really want a Sprite."

"No, a REAL drink. My treat," his persistence gaining an edge of indignation.

Utterly amused by his frustration, I mimicked him, "I understand. But I don't drink, so WHAT I REALLY. WANT. IS. A. SPRITE."

Mitch smiled at me, recognizing the absurdity of the exchange, how the man was completely derailed by my responses. A perplexed crease formed between Ben's eyebrows, and he lowered himself from the tiptoes I hadn't noticed he was standing on. He removed his arms from our shoulders and stepped away toward the bar behind us, never returning with my Sprite.

I laughed out loud and smiled at Mitch. How peculiar it was that this man was so emphatic about buying us a drink, but completely lost when I answered with my request for soda. It was unexpected but saying "no" felt so good. Here I was, a people-pleaser who rarely said "no," now claiming my place in an alcohol-free life, and each time felt like redemption surging through my bones. I tossed out all the social norms and expectations I had lived my life trying so hard to obey. Happy hours, champagne toasts, a glass of wine to take the edge off, a beer to cry into. Instead, I was living each day with a blank slate to imagine a new way of living for myself.

I kept trying new things. I started reading and writing again like I did when I was younger. I took up macramé and gardening. Mitch and I went on more bike rides and weekend getaways, making new memories to mark the change. We would park next to the frozen lake so we could stay warm in our car as we watched the sunset, protected from the cold winter's air. Afterward, we would cruise the neighborhood to take in the remaining holiday lights. As I shared the unfolding journey with others, it became easier each and every day.

Each day I took a moment to ask myself, *What do you need today?* If I was tired, I cozied up with a warm blanket and took a nap. If I needed more help with sober tips and tricks, I returned to the memoirs and recovery podcasts. When I needed nature, Mitch and I would grab our mountain bikes and retreat to the woods for a few hours, stopping to take pictures of all the beautiful things we would see while we were out. If I felt overwhelmed, I would take a long hot shower with my eyes closed, and focused on the feeling of the warm water as it rolled gently over my skin.

Before bed, we would take a moment to celebrate the count of days, "Today was day ten. It's day fifteen. Twenty-two!"

"Keep it up, Kristy Kreme," Mitch would say as he embraced me, another victory along the way.

All these changes were minute and new, yet they were monumental and impactful, everything I needed to get through each day. I reflected and began molding my life into one I was excited to live. I no longer wanted to live my life full of regret that I couldn't drink any longer. I was building a life where I no longer wanted to drink. I wanted to be sober. I wanted to be free.

I was becoming the phoenix, rising from the ashes of my past now smarter, mightier, and more powerful than ever before. Fierce and luminous, I forged a new life in recovery.

Waves

What if I come out different?
What if you do?
What if you don't love me anymore,
or if I don't?

—A letter to my husband after one month sober

* * *

There is something about waves that crash or caress the shore
that speaks to me without words. A recognition I find deep
inside, the tides pulling at the emotions as they churn within
me. I have stood before the ocean with my eyes closed, anxiety escaping as I breathed out, relaxing as the waves pulled
my tension out to sea. Evenings were spent watching gentle
ripples on a calm lake during a summer storm, soothed by
the way it remains at peace as rain collides against its surface.

In college, I stood on the shores of Lake Superior on an anniversary of the Edmund Fitzgerald shipwreck, the most famous
wreck in Superior's history. That day, twenty-three years later,

gale force winds whipped across the lake as intensely as they had the fateful night it sank. The cold November windstorm pelted my face with ice that rolled in with the tide as I stood on her shore. With feet planted on slippery stones and eyes clenched, I listened as the waves exploded violently against the boulders on the rocky shoreline. Inside, my heart was being tossed in the turbulent nervousness that left me constantly picking at my cuticles, mounting pressure in school, slammed by the dense weight of my homesickness.

The harsh windchill bit at my cheeks and tears froze the corners of my lashes together, leaving me to force them open each time I looked back out over the raging water. I cried on her shore hoping the waves would take my sadness, burying it in the darkest depths of her frigid waters.

My silent distress signal to no one, too afraid to call for help.

* * *

In all the books I read and podcasts I listened to focused on sobriety and recovery, every single one of them mentioned emotions coming back months after getting sober. The sentiment was overarching and unanimously confirmed, leaving me perplexed by how it could possibly be true. I had spent my whole life in a whirlpool of emotional chaos. It was the core disturbance I drank to suppress.

How could there possibly be more?

Right on schedule, a couple months into sobriety, the emotions I submerged in booze began to resurface. Fidgeting turned into pacing and quickly derailed into fiery outbursts of mundane annoyances. The socks on the floor, the stack of unopened mail. It was harmless yet my reactions were unstable and surprising even to me. Feelings of anger rolled in leaving guilt and regret behind in their wake. I felt raw and vulnerable every second of the day. Exposed, nerves firing unexpectedly. Although the silence in my mind and the healthy changes in my body were celebrated daily, it wasn't enough to tame the agitation that still lingered.

Drinking was a steady oppression of my emotions. I drank alcohol to smother my distress, never learning how to process feelings I didn't understand. I choked down my emotions with shots of candy flavored liqueur losing years of speaking up about what I was going through, maturing without the ability to define myself or life's peculiar experiences. Years of not learning about boundaries and gaining the courage to fight for them.

So much time was lost on false beliefs. I thought wine could numb all the "bad" feelings and let me embrace only the "good" ones. As if it could identify them at a molecular level and dispose of them appropriately. But alcohol is not that sophisticated. Even pain killers don't operate with such precision. All that time, I was really just shutting off the most honest piece of myself. I was ignoring the truths inside me, the person I was born to be. Sadly, I believed life would be better if I was someone else.

Sober... I had nowhere to hide.

Two months after I quit drinking, Mitch got a call from his brother and, by the immediate fade of his smile, I knew something was wrong. He put the call on speaker phone, and I heard Max on the other end of the line. He had just spoken with their aunt back home who said their mom was dying. Max was flying out first thing the next morning.

"We'll meet you there," Mitch replied with a gruff hitch in his voice. I placed my hand on his shoulder and started a packing list in my head.

Betty lived in a quaint memory care facility a few blocks from the home Mitch and Max grew up in. She was in her late seventies and needed full-time care and supervision as her mind slowly deteriorated, no longer capable of caring for herself. She had stopped eating and was getting weaker, so we found a dog sitter for Rosco and packed the car. We drove south to meet Max the next morning. Staring out the windshield during the five-hour drive, a thought drifted in on occasion that I pushed aside every time: *Is this how I relapse?*

We met up with Max in the parking lot of Betty's home, exchanging pained glances and tight bear hugs. I followed the two men into the softly lit room where she laid silently in her twin bed. Betty's sister sat on the side of the bed like a sentinel, raising her eyes to greet us with a pained smile as we neared them. We had just seen Betty four months before, dining on her favorite hard-shell tacos as we told her stories of bike races and shared pictures of our latest road trip adventure. She was alert and smiling back then. But now Betty was frail and thin, laying peacefully on her side wrapped in warm blankets, the oxygen machine humming at her bedside.

"She smiled yesterday when I told her you were coming," their aunt reassured us quietly. In the soft light from the bedside lamp, Betty's eyes were closed, and she moved just slightly as we settled into chairs close to the bed. We took turns holding her delicate hands and greeting her. We embraced each tiny movement as a sign she knew we were there.

The hum of the oxygen tank disappeared as I stared at Betty, so different from the woman I had seen before. Betty, who always wore blue unless there was a University of Iowa home game, the only time she decked herself out in head-to-toe Hawkeye gear. Who dug out a book on manners when it came to planning Mitch's and my wedding, insisting we get it right. Betty, a self-made woman who had the heart and tenacity to be a teacher, a mother, a devoted wife, and sister.

She welcomed me into her home with a hug the day I met her, only having been with Mitch a few months. She gave us a handwritten recipe book so we could make all her favorite recipes, a vegan cake, and an indulgently savory dilly bread. Betty taught me the magic of shopping the Von Maur clearance shoe room and all the delights we would find. She had the grace years prior to pick out the perfect dress for me to wear to her husband's funeral when I was too overwhelmed to find one for myself.

As the pain rolled in like waves, I was washed with gratitude that we had made it in time to be by her side. There was nowhere else in the world we needed to be other than right there in that moment. We stayed throughout the day, leaving only to grab dinner and return so Mitch could remain at her side through the night. Before I left, I held Betty's fragile hand in mine one more time. "I love you, Betty. It's okay if you need to go," I said and held a sob down as I hugged Mitch goodbye.

I drove Max back to the hotel we were all staying at. "Mitch will call if anything changes," I told him as we stood outside the side entrance. "If he calls, I'll wake you up. Just try to get some sleep." We parted and I tossed my things on the floor the moment I walked into my room. Rather than pour myself a glass of wine as I had done each time before, I brewed bed-time tea, put on my pajamas, and crawled into bed.

When Mitch's dad was dying of cancer years prior, Mitch, Betty and I slept on cots in his hospice room. We took turns by his side during the day, playing music and telling him stories. By evening, we would try to sleep by the twinkling of heart monitors and exit signs. I couldn't fathom grief then, drinking burgundy wine from a plastic hospital cup, sitting quietly on my cot as Betty and Mitch slept in their beds beside me.

In our hotel room alone and away from everything, I cried for my mother-in-law until my tears subsided, falling asleep with a damp pillowcase and cellphone in my hand.

The phone rang just after one o'clock in the morning.

When I answered, I could hear crying on the other end of the phone, and I knew immediately she was gone. "I'm on my way, baby. I am so sorry, I love you," was all I could say. I hung up with him and called Max, waking him from slumber with news I never wanted to be the one to give. We made a plan to meet at the car in ten minutes so we could get ourselves together before we left. I stood in the bathroom as I brushed the sleep from my eyes and grief settled into my heart.

As the sadness closed in on me, a sliver of comfort momentarily caught my attention. Next to my sorrow sat the tiny, powerful voice inside me waving, calling attention to a little spark, recognizing not a single part of me wanted a drink in that moment. Not one ounce. It didn't feel real. *Maybe it's the time of day? Maybe I'm just too sleepy. It's strange, but I really don't want one.*

I gathered my things and left to meet Max by the car. His signature feet-off-the-ground hug was a little more earthbound this time, lingering as the loss of Betty became increasingly more real. While the old me would have drank until I passed out, waking at this hour still drunk and driving back to Betty's place on high-alert, this time was different. This time I was sober. I was clearheaded and on a mission to get Max to see his mother. I was determined to be there for Mitch.

By the time we arrived, Mitch had alerted the staff and was growing weary after sitting awake with his mother through her final hours. I kissed her forehead and said a final goodbye to the woman who always made me feel like family, felt my heart shudder, and break into millions of tiny pieces. Max took over, calling the funeral home and hospice team as I drove Mitch back to our hotel room to sleep.

As we laid in the darkness, I held him until he drifted off. His slow breathing comforted me as I tried to wrestle with my own heartache, trying to accept it, to sit with it, without pushing it away. The grief was quiet and still, as if the seconds forgot to tick by. Waves of agony were accompanied by mists of happy memories. I remembered her excitement when we would bring her Belgian waffles for breakfast on weekend trips to see her. I could hear her voice when she said "I love you" the last time I hugged her goodbye, tasting metal on my tongue like copper as if my cells couldn't contain the grief either.

Like a ship wreck at the bottom of the sea, I sat in stillness, felt the pressure holding me in place, until I settled into my own slumber. Dreams of Betty played all night long.

After Betty's funeral, Mitch, Max, his wife Allie, and I went out to a glitzy restaurant to celebrate her life. Max ordered a bottle of wine and four glasses and I immediately looked at Mitch in protest. "Just a sip doesn't count," he whispered to answer the fears painted across my face. When the bottle was delivered to the table, Max poured three full glasses and a splash into the fourth glass which he pushed over to me. I felt a hesitant tremor in my hand as I put my fingers on the stem and pulled it close.

"To Betty," we said in unison as we raised our glasses in her honor. I held the glass up to my mouth and tipped it until the red wine touched my lips.

You don't have to drink it.

The whisper was soft in my heart and it immediately felt as if Betty was there by my side, reassuring me, strengthening me against my own uncertainty. Maybe it was my own inner voice. It didn't matter. I lowered my glass without drinking it and pushed it over to Mitch. He squeezed my hand below the table and drank the swallow on my behalf. I raised my mocktail and smiled and took a drink to thank her for everything she was to me. Then and now.

In my heart, I celebrated a major victory, feeling invincible, as if putting that glass down broke me out of chains I couldn't see. I was no longer worried I would never get to drink again. It was the unexpected magic of realizing I *didn't have to.*

* * *

Within weeks of Betty's funeral, the COVID-19 pandemic had spread to the US and mass shutdowns were rolling across the country. My employer sent us all home for two weeks but, having watched the international news for months, I grabbed all my things as if I'd been let go. I knew we wouldn't be coming back any time soon. Weeks turned into months, yoga pants turned into regular work attire, and we found ways to adapt to a new world of social distancing.

Alcohol consumption was on the rise in the US and liquor stores were considered essential businesses in Minnesota along with hospitals, grocers, and public transportation. This allowed them to stay open while most other businesses were barred from opening their doors. Alcohol and drug-related deaths rose dramatically in the first year, increasing by 25.5 percent for alcohol, opioid deaths by 40.8 percent, and deaths by drugs like fentanyl surged 59 percent over previous years (White et al 2022). The stress and anxiety of the global pandemic left no one unscathed.

In our cozy home, I tried to view the social distancing as welcome seclusion, an opportunity to celebrate all the cancelled social obligations I feared would challenge me in early sobriety. I spent the extra time reading and listening to my podcasts. Mitch and I rode our bikes together daily and took Rosco for more walks than his little legs asked for. When the social uprisings and riots happened after the murder of George Floyd, we partnered with our neighbors to protect our block at night as rioters burned dumpsters just blocks from our home. I tried to calm myself when the haunting sounds of police helicopters circled overhead.

Through the uncertainty, fear, injustice, and turmoil that surrounded us, memories of my past transgressions continued to surface and challenge my grip on the world around me. Drunken escapades I had forgotten, ghosts I thought had disappeared, and shame I never got over came crashing over me like tidal waves in the confines of our little condo. They refused to wane or retreat. For the first time in our fourteen years together, it registered with me that I rarely ever shared my true feelings with Mitch. With anyone. I had run from them or drank them away my whole life, and now I had to find a new way to deal with this very real part of me. I had to find a way to weather the storm or sink.

As emotions resurfaced, I shook with frustration, barely knowing how to name each one as they crashed against my shores. Humor tasted like a delicacy on my tongue, an indulgence to share with Mitch and a couple mischievous grins. Anger landed hard against me, leaving feelings of shame and remorse as the tides pulled my rage back down below the surface. When sobriety felt effortless and I lost track of my counting of days, guilt over the ease of it washed against my tender edges and I fought to retain my grip on the bliss of it.

I held onto my gratitude for sobriety like an anchor, fearful that my emotional turbulence would drive him away. Although I was gaining confidence in who I was becoming, I worried that the new me wouldn't be someone Mitch could still love. Yet each day he was there to hold me when I cried. To celebrate another day sober with candlelit dinners and nonalcoholic rosé. To laugh along next to me as we killed the hours with old movies and fresh cookies from the oven.

I was done running from my past, done escaping myself. I no longer wanted to live as I had all my life, keeping everyone at arm's length, never connecting at a soulful level. My lack of healthy relationships and vibrant, human connections wasn't because I was a bad person. I simply never let anyone in. I protected myself by making everyone disposable. Cut them out of my life before they could leave me. The same fear I always believed about myself: I was forgettable. Replaceable. No one of note.

I no longer wanted to run away and start over. I was proud of the decisions I was making and was beginning to like the woman I was becoming. This was my chance to find relief from my troubles now, just as I am. To turn into the storm without numbing the pain.

Surviving the Fires

———

I often joke that I like my coffee "as black as my soul." Similar to most people I know who make tough jokes about mental health, I'm only ever half kidding. I don't mean "black as my soul" in a demonic way. I love black coffee. And I do believe that my soul has a decent amount of smoldering char to it. For most of my life it seemed like at least one part of my existence was in a constant state of uncontrolled burn, narrow pillars of white smoke rising from the ashes, still hot from the latest fire.

Scarred from the flames that came before it. Somehow I still made it out alive.

In areas prone to frequent forest fires, many species of trees have adapted to survive the destructive flames, living on amidst the rubble after the flames run out of fuel. The ponderosa pine, for example, can persist in regions with frequent, "low-intensity surface fires" due to the thicker bark it developed. The deep, flaky hull prevents fires from reaching the inner layers of the tree where it stores all its nutrients and water, allowing it to thrive once the fires subside (Mullen 2017).

Alcohol was the forest fire in the wilderness of my life. Constantly burned by the intensity and heat. Each phase of my relationship with alcohol taught me new ways to endure and, eventually, sobriety would allow me to flourish. In my teens and twenties, my relationship with alcohol felt like small, frequent fires igniting the world around me. Rather than maturing, I was clawing through my own attempts at survival, growing thicker skin and reinforcing the walls I built around my heart. I enclosed myself in a fortress to protect against pain and rejection, thick walls holding the blaze at bay. Surviving back then required me to out outlast the fires, be tough, and move on.

When my alcohol addiction intensified in my thirties, the expanse of the fires stretched out in every direction. Whatever I was trying to avoid, grief, anxiety, anger, self-doubt, everything I thought alcohol helped me handle was a lie. I woke every morning with a burning hatred for myself lodged in the center of my chest, flames licking at my heart and mind. The all-consuming blaze kept part of me focused on my addiction at all times. Little remained of my focus and energy to live the rest of my life with any sense of purpose. With one foot pointed toward my next drink, the next inferno, it was hard to point myself in the direction I wanted to go. I needed to burn all my false beliefs to the ground so I could learn to thrive, not just survive, in sobriety.

The shortleaf pine has a similar survival strategy, using an extensive root system that allows it to evade death after complete scorching of the above-ground growth. The wide-reaching roots hold small underground buds that lie dormant until needed then utilize the nutrients in the roots to sprout new trees. Rising through the burnt forest floor, the small pines emerge as new life to begin the cycle again. Fresh, green, and soaking up light to help it grow.

When I changed my mindset, when I took an honest look at why alcohol held such power over me, it was like awakening dormant bulbs below ground. With a thirst for knowledge and a will to prevail, I stretched and grew and found a way to bloom as I rose from the ashes of my own undoing.

* * *

A year into my sobriety and the COVID lockdowns, my employer rolled out a major initiative to offer weekly mental health and wellbeing resources to all its staff and their families. We received invites to online meditation classes, free virtual workout websites, and monthly speakers who taught us about self-care and navigating the pandemic. Being newly sober, the extra focus on wellbeing was a welcome new work perk.

We were offered free online resources to help with anxiety. They sent care packages of teas and chocolates to our homes, and the chefs in our vacant cafeteria hosted virtual baking classes for the holidays. My favorite was the virtual fireside chats between our C-suite executives and authors and visionaries focused on personal growth. Thought-provoking interviews with authors like Adam Grant and Glennon Doyle.

The butter-smooth poetry of Tabitha Brown's cooking class that tied every ingredient to love and self-care.

Deepak Chopra, mental-health advocate and author, joined one of our executives for a discussion from his home centered around gratitude and mindfulness. I was still struggling to move beyond just *not drinking alcohol*. I went to every mental health expert's virtual discussion, every meditation class and stretching breaks offered, longing for the next key to my recovery. I needed to learn how to move on from my addiction and begin to heal.

I curled up in my robin's egg blue office chair, Betty's favorite color, with my feet in fuzzy socks tucked under my tush. With my camera off, I sipped slowly on a lavender hot tea in my t-shirt and flannel pants. I waited for the chat to begin, glancing around at the teal walls of my home office, and smiled. *How lucky am I to get this opportunity through work?* Not only to see Deepak, but I was grateful for the advantage of listening to him from the privacy of my own home, free to openly cry in the safety of my own space.

Deepak was poised on a plush white chair in his home. The image mixed with his silvery voice made the experience more intimate and informal than I imagined possible. He spoke with our EVP empathetically about the collective grief felt across the globe for not only the loss of life, but the loss of the world as we knew it. He shared the benefits of gratitude, meditation, and mindfulness in times of difficulty and also in the enjoyment of everyday life. I turned up the volume, filling my home office with the peacefulness of his voice.

"When you are feeling grateful," he explained, "it's impossible to feel hostile or victimized at the same time." I practiced my morning gratitude journaling for more than a year. Somedays, I wrote heartfelt sentiments with doodles of hearts and smiley faces. Others were more practical, succinct. *I am grateful for fresh coffee.* Hearing him speak so beautifully about the emotional and scientific benefits of it made it feel immensely more powerful to me. It felt validating, like I was doing something positive for myself for a change.

They covered the mental health benefits of meditation, Chopra leaning into the importance of taking it one step further with mindfulness. Mindfulness is the practice of giving attention, observing, and being present at any given moment. The focus turns to the senses, the sound of air rustling through the trees, the smell of freshly cut grass or the aftertaste of your morning coffee. Witnessing the changing feelings in the body as different thoughts or feelings arise, tensions and twitches, burning ears and furrowed brow. Mindfulness is simply observing their arrival and allowing them to float by.

My eyes flittered across the framed pictures on my turquoise walls. *Just float by...*

He was poetic as he described the uniqueness of every given moment. Mindfulness, he described, allows us to be present for the simple miracle of its uniqueness. "Your heart is beating without any effort, my body is healing without any effort, it's all a miracle!" Deepak smiled with energy as he pronounced "miracle," his hands steepled in front of him as he sat relaxed in his chair.

It brought to mind how every week I maintained my sobriety, the more my body healed in unexpected ways. My taste buds changed, and I fell in love with the flavor of Mitch's home-cooked steaks. Oddly, all pork products tasted like hot dogs to me for a few months but luckily that eventually passed, and I was able to enjoy bacon again. The puffiness of my face subsided, adding definition to my cheekbones and bringing out the dimples I forgot I had.

I had it all wrong before that day. I meditated each week to chase all the racing thoughts from my mind. I tried to sit in silence but they were always there, the unrelenting ghosts, the memories of days I'd buried long ago. They came to me as if the tape was playing backward, from my final days of drinking back to my origins of regret. I remember the shame I felt from blacking out on Thanksgiving. The Louisville luchadors and throwing up all over the side of the car. I saw faces of people I ran from, glances of disappointment from Mitch, countless memories that almost destroyed me.

They met me in meditation, exposing that I was walking around with unhealed wounds all my life. As they dove deeper into their conversation on my screen, I knew *my* heart continued to beat without effort, my body was healing as well.

He emphasized how important it is to acknowledge the experiences, ideas, and feelings without judgment. Chopra taught us to bear witness to the thoughts and emotions that flit into mind and draw our attention "with awareness, choice, and compassion."

Compassion. Nonjudgment. The final missing pieces.

I devoured each of Deepak's words, flowing like silk as the miles that separated us seemed to melt away. From a corner of my room, it floated in from the ether and I watched it go by... *Kristy, we made it to forty years old.* I was more than a year sober and getting stronger every day. *That* was my miracle. Tears rolled down my face and I raised my arms in celebration.

The hour-long conversation about healing and growing ended with a guided meditation and he sent us back to our day with one last nugget of hope I would sew into my routine. He reminded us how our time in quarantine and social distancing was an "opportunity to reinvent our bodies and resurrect our souls. Let us focus on total wellbeing." It was apparent to me that I needed to keep taking care of myself if I was going to learn how to move forward.

After watching the interview that day, I tried to keep compassion close at hand when uncomfortable moods arose. What started as awkward and odd at first became cleansing and tranquil as "sitting with your feelings" became a new bloom of understanding within me. The more I was able to acknowledge the shame or anxiety that appeared in my life and accept it purely as a part of me, the less impact it had on my day.

Rather than running from each recurring memory, I began to let them come to me in search of what I needed to see. Before, I thought I needed to figure out a way to forgive myself for my behavior, for my choices, and the mistakes I made. But it wasn't forgiveness I was waiting for. The real key to my recovery would be a simple act of humanity.

I stopped trying to understand why I did things and focused on sympathizing with the younger versions of me instead, giving myself kindness and tenderness for the first time in my life. Looking at myself without judgment brought me closer to knowing myself as the sensitive, complex human being I was. I silenced my inner critic by focusing on not reacting emotionally to the memories that appeared in my mind. It allowed me to grow and heal from all the false-beliefs I had constructed throughout my life.

What I didn't expect was, as I learned how to accept my struggles and fears, the magnitude and bounty of joy I found grew exponentially. I stopped questioning whether it was socially acceptable to be happy in the middle of a global pandemic. Every moment of delight flooded the holes within me I had always tried to fill with wine. Learning to let down my guard and stop waiting for the other shoe to drop, for the bottom to fall out, allowed contentment to illuminate each day with a mellow, amber glow.

I started embracing all the things in life that made me feel alive, whether they were big or small. Frosting cookies and planting flowers. Finally getting the promotion and paying off debts with money saved by not drinking. Memories about getting drunk at Jenny's cabin roused my humiliation. But dancing in the kitchen and singing along to the sixties soul and R&B music that her family turned me onto allowed me to exchange the embarrassment with contentment. Honoring the discomfort as I looked back on them with compassion and love instead, I found a way to be grateful for every crevasse formed in me along the way.

I still knew every word to the songs I loved so long ago.

* * *

In regions where the forest fires spread rapidly with accelerated heat and intensity, trees have adapted to keep future generations safe rather than protecting itself. Pines such as the Jack pine or table mountain pine grow "serotinous" cones, extremely thick and solid cones sealed with a natural resin that protects the seeds, prevailing unopened for years on the tree. Only under the intense heat of a blaze will the resin melt, allowing the cone to open and seeds to fall to the scorched earth below or be carried off on a passing wind.

Many times in early sobriety, staying mindful in a moment felt like being a seed held protected inside a Jack pine cone. As my emotions and memories flared and burned around me, I held steady inside my safe space, watching the swirling flames dance around me. Once the heat and flares of my past tore through my life and my memories, the resin that held me in place melted away, allowing me to step out on my own.

Whether I fell or floated this time, it was a new beginning either way.

Bonneville

———

I had always thought sobriety was just about *not drinking*. Recovery was a vague, undetermined amount of time you remained freaked out and skittish. And addicted was forever.

But now, I knew getting sober meant more than just saying "no" to alcohol. Addiction wasn't just the constant presence of alcohol in life, but my dependence on it. We addicts rely on it to treat parts of our life it was never intended to cure. Recovery was a multifaceted process by which addiction could become a thing of the past. I had never imagined the final secret to my recovery would open the doors to most of the mysteries of my life.

A year and a half into my sobriety, Mitch and I ventured off on a spring road trip to Santa Rosa, California, to visit friends. The restrictions from the COVID-19 pandemic were finally easing back and travel was once again resuming. We needed an adventure as much as the next person. Needed a chance to stretch our legs, take a deep breath and relax.

We broke up the thirty-hour drive into two sections, stopping to sleep for a night in Salt Lake City, Utah, after an aggressive eighteen-hour first shift. Mitch did most of the driving as I nodded off into bouts of light sleep. We spent the night in a quiet hotel to grab a warm shower and rest before venturing out for the final twelve-hour pull. We loaded up the car then turned out the lights in our room the next morning, quietly checking out just before 5:30 a.m. The city lights twinkled in the remaining darkness of night.

We had already ticked off more than half the total drive from Minnesota but there was still a layer of the last eighteen months clinging to me. I felt stuck, as if something was mysteriously barring me from completely relaxing. The pandemic, riots, lockdowns, working from home, trying to stay sober through it all. It lingered, irritating my chest like a hair stuck to the inside of your shirt. You can't see it so you paw at your breasts, run your nails down the fabric, annoyed as you try to find it. I stared into the darkness just beyond our headlights and tried to simply breathe.

All the authors I leaned on to move beyond my addiction wrote about the contentment found in sober living. I believed it was out there, but I suffered from pangs of guilt for having made it this far. A thick cloak blanketed me, stifled my happiness, still hindering me from breathing deeply. It left me afflicted not by the absence of alcohol, but by the ease I found in sobriety this time around. I was doing all the work to make my sober living simple and pleasant, yet somehow I still felt remorse for getting it right.

I watched in the side mirror as faint silhouettes of the mountains rose behind us like sleepy giants rustled awake by the impending sun. A hint of the predawn light exposed their massive size as I stared. We drove across the flat, barren Bonneville Salt Flats as the waxing sunlight revealed stories of lives that passed through there before us. Sand sculptures of serpents and sharks jumped out of the salty, cracked ground alongside tire tracks and remnants of bonfires that had long since burned out.

I stared silently out the passenger window, taking in hand-laid rock formations that spelled out words for passersby to witness.

HOPE
JOY
LOVE

I read each one, mentally caressing the words as they passed through my mind. Like a whispered truth, a carnal longing within us all, the velvety messages revealing themselves in the predawn light.

Just before the sun broke over the horizon behind us, we pulled into the final Bonneville rest stop where a few small groups of people had gathered to watch the sunrise. Mitch navigated our minivan out onto the salt flats and the air at the horizon vibrated with the growing light.

"Mitch, the sun is rising. NOW!"

Mitch already had one foot on the ground before he put the van in park. The sun peeked up above the horizon where the mountains descended to the earth. We sprang from the car, stopping side by side to face the rising sun as it overtook the night sky.

It was breathtaking.

The cold wind gusted and swirled, stirring something inside of me, stealing my breath and replacing it with icy air that shocked my lungs. The colors were magnificent as they spread across the heavens. I didn't try to stop myself as I began to cry.

I gasped, the air inside me yanked toward the sun, feeling as though it stole a piece of me with it. That part of me still frozen in the struggle of my addiction to alcohol. Abruptly ripped from my bosom to be exposed for what it was, a barricade that didn't know it was time to go. My chest heaved in the release as one moment unfolded into the next.

The emerging sun climbed and burned brighter, not waiting for the world's approval or readiness for its arrival. It didn't ask for permission. It simply stretched and filled the sky to become the shining light it was always meant to be. I watched with new eyes, a fresh perspective, as my throat tightened, and warm tears fell from my lower lids. Magnificent energy swirled powerfully within me, an awakening, a reconnection to the light inside myself.

The sun took shape as the violet and navy blue sky melted into fiery oranges and magenta hues. Those brief moments felt like an eternity's worth of understanding unfolded within me. With every breath and quiver of my chin, I felt a release happen within me. It was the first time I felt a true understanding of myself settle in.

I finally released myself from the shame of becoming addicted. I let go of my guilt over getting sober, tired of running and exhausted from suppressing myself. Living alcohol-free was fine, but I wanted more. I wanted to live in celebration of my sobriety. To rejoice in who I've become. Break free the goofy, hopeful dreamer who was inside of me all along. Unapologetically Me, shining brightly for all to see.

I closed my eyes, and it was just me, the sunrise, and the frigid air in my lungs.

I caught Mitch looking back at me from the photo he was taking when I reopened my eyes. His long legs closed the short distance between us in a few strides when he saw the dampness of my cheeks. He pulled me into his arms, and I laid my head on his chest as we both looked out at the glorious skyline, breathing in sync.

We took one last picture of the sunrise and hopped back in the van headed toward Nevada. I sat quietly for the first few miles, reliving the experience on repeat in my mind, letting my thoughts wonder as they wished. I felt released, cleansed. A deliverance from who I used to be.

I watched the desert landscape brighten with the morning sun, illuminating its vastness. I sat in silence with my thoughts about what I'd gone through to get to this point in my sobriety. The memories of hard experiences I had faced.

Blackouts, disappointments, and piles of regrets. I remembered the mistakes I had to take ownership of. The time with the people I love that I had lost. There was endless sadness for all the years I spent buried in my own shit, in so deep I could never really be there for my friends and family. How I could never truly connect with others because I spent so much time guarding myself, unable to see past my own efforts to survive.

Those fires that burned and scarred me.

The music disappeared into the background of my thoughts as Mitch drove. Wading through all the memories, all the versions of me that had come before, I finally saw them for who they were at the time. I stopped condemning their mistakes, stopped measuring their worth, choosing instead to acknowledge how each one contributed to the woman I am now. I finally found a way to look at myself without judgment and accept myself for exactly who I was. Flaws, cracks, industrial-strength glue, and all.

One year, four months, and sixteen days sober until I finally learned how to stop judging myself.

I was new and the same all at once. And I realized that I loved her, I loved Me, exactly how I was. *Why on earth would I ever want to go back to living the life I had been living?* There was no longer a fear of what the world could throw at me to make me want to drink again. Instead, just a reassuring knowing that I never had to. Never again.

* * *

Somewhere down the road in Nevada, as we watched the sun-drenched landscape whir by, "Me & Julio Down by the Schoolyard" by Paul Simon began playing on the satellite radio. It has always been one of those songs that instantly returns me to my childhood, singing it word for word with my dad in his old Ford pickup truck. He smiled when he sang it and I loved to see him smile. The tender memory pulled at the corners of my mouth as the recognizable acoustic guitar riff pulled at the younger me inside. As soon as Simon started in about Mama Pajama, I was singing along at the top of my lungs as Mitch kept us steered toward California.

Line after line, the more I sang, the more my chest expanded and filled with air. In between the words, I found a lightness inside me building. Joy, love, and hope had somehow jumped onboard when I wasn't looking, and I smiled once I finally noticed them.

"Keep going, this is the cutest thing ever!" Mitch said as his smile grew along with my own. *How had I closed myself off so far that I didn't even sing in front of my own husband?* I never did. Not like this. I couldn't remember the last time I felt this free and light.

We sang together to the Beastie Boys, Jimi Hendrix, and Neil Young. We told each other new stories from our childhoods, laughed and crooned together more than ever before. What amazing times we could have had all those years. It was a somber reminder that I hadn't been my true self for way too long. As I stared over the highway before us, I let the sadness swirl around me, hovering above my skin. As it danced in the light, I tried to understand it without pulling it down inside of me.

I was sad that I had lost myself so long ago.
How many years had I wasted trying to shield myself from pain?
How much growth, learning, connection had I lost out on?
How had anyone ever have loved the vacant shell of a human I had become?

The next fifty miles passed in a blink, taking the sadness with it, leaving me relaxed and serene. *If this is what sober living is like, I don't ever want to go back.* I rolled the window down and the arid desert air filled my nose as the heat spilled into our van. I fished my hand up and down slowly in the stream of hot air passing my window. Smiling a toothy Cheshire grin that strained my cheeks, eyes closed, I tipped my head back and released myself from my restraints. I let go of all the tension I forgot to put down once I got sober, finally dropping all the baggage I'd already made room for on sunlit shelves of my past.

I have never agreed with the adage, "You can't love anyone until you learn to love yourself." Bullshit. You can love other people while hating yourself, it's how I managed the first forty years of my life. The real secret I never could have imagined, the infinite beauty, is the magnificent depths of love you can expand into once you truly learn to love yourself.

Ever since Mitch started teaching me how to mountain bike sixteen years ago, he has always shouted out words of encouragement along each ride. "Good climb, Kristy! Eyes up. You can do this." Sometimes I was embarrassed, as if he was calling attention to my weaknesses I didn't want anyone else to see. But after the sunrise in Bonneville, I heard his words for the first time with my heart.

"Full pull!" Mitch hollered as I successfully completed a very technical climb without taking my feet off the pedals once we reached the West coast. This time, the words excited me, sent tingles down to my toes. It was just the two of us out riding in nature, shouting joyfully as we played bikes in the California sun. It felt like I was feeling the genuine depths of his love for the very first time.

One of my favorite authors, Brené Brown wrote, "True belonging doesn't require us to change who we are; it requires us to be who we are" (Brown 2021). Now, I couldn't agree more. Coming out of the Bonneville sunrise, I worked to understand myself and all my intricate, raw, and exquisite emotions. It allowed me to connect with the people in my life in a way I had never experienced. I could be present for hours of tough conversations without worrying if I'd be able to leave in time to get to the liquor store before it closed. I remembered every holiday, concert, and sunset that came and went. I cried every tear and turned every laugh up to eleven, allowing them to burst out into the world.

Today, life is full of music playing in many rooms of our home. I'm dancing to Sam Cooke and Etta James in my kitchen as I bake cookies for the fifth or sixth time each week. I talk to Mitch and Rosco in my best "Roseanne Roseannadanna" voice. *Thank you, Gilda Radner!* And sometimes, I break her out with my friends, too. I smile until my face hurts, I cry until my heart is ready to stop, and I rejoice as often as I can. The connection I feel in every cell in my body is electric and alive.

Here in my sobriety, I finally found the alchemy of my soul I always yearned for.

I found peace.
I found
hope,
joy,
and love.

All My Love and Gratitude...

My endless gratitude goes out to my husband for keeping me fed, giving me extra hugs along the way, and getting me out on fun date nights while I worked long hours to bring this dream to life. I'm blessed with your strength and optimism, empowered by your infinite love and support. xoxo

To my amazing team at New Degree Press and Manuscripts: Kasey Kubica, my brave and encouraging editor, thank you for trusting me when I said each chapter needed to be rewritten. You gave me the opportunity to dig out the real story I wanted to tell. To my marketing guru George Thorne, you turned the stressful, scary part of promoting myself and my work into a more fun and playful adventure that I could enjoy. To my editor, Katie Sigler, thank you for helping me find my words and opening my world to some amazing new authors. Thank you Kyra Ann Dawkins, Reilly Vore, Shanna Heath, Sherman Morrison, and Eric Koester for all the amazing things you taught me along the way!

To my author friends who kept me accountable, shared their wisdom and encouraging words, I'm so happy to have you on my side. Thank you, Robin Voreis, Maggie Smith, Shirley Muñoz Newson, Phil Van Valkenberg, Cory Mortenson, Michele Schalin, Naomi Vladeck, Janna Brayman, and Pavita Singh.

To my beta readers, thank you for your time and thoughtful feedback when I asked for your help! Thank you, Morgan Sylvester, Mary Randleman, Kaveh Rahimi, Sarah Pritzker, Kit Oslin, Amy Ochs, Cory Mortensen, Megan Morley, Sheila LaVigne, Leslie Kegel, Jodie Karjala, Faith Jalas, Martha Flynn Kauth, Randy Engebritson, Bonny Donzella, Angela Carlson, Lisa Britton, and Cheryl Barker.

For my amazing author community who has helped me through the writing process with your support and generosity during my presale campaign, you helped make this dream come true! Thank you for believing in me, Ashley Ackerson, Tim Anderson, Josh Anderson, Cheryl Barker, Todd & Kellie Bauer, Lindsay Berg, Ginny Betzer, Tim Brandvold, Aimee Brask, Lisa Britton, Dana Buddenbaum, Kate & Cory Mortensen, Mark Butcher, Kate Callahan, Amy Campbell, Angela Carlson, Cindy Christian, Susan Conley, Jessica Constant, Gary Crandall, Christopher Cross, Eileen Cummings, Holly DeLisi, Bonny Donzella, Randy Engebritson, Jennifer & Cj Faulkner, Megan Felling, Jeanne Fleck, Martha Flynn, Linda jean Fobian, Nancy & Ron Gallas, Michelle Gomez, Julie Gujer, Leslie Hale, Natalie Hale, Tess Hayes, John Henderson, Jay Henderson, Joy Herzog, Delsie Hoffey, Shad Holland, Arik Holm, Autumn Hughes, Kristen Iburg-Meyer, Jane IntVeldt, Brian Jablonski, Faith Jalas,

Shirley Johnson, Dana Johnson, Carol Jordan, Georgia Kaftan, Jodie Karjala, Eddie Karow, Leslie Kegel, Tom Kendall, Suzanne Klein, Eric Koester, Karin Kopish, Jacquelyn Kozak, David Krattley, Sheila LaVigne, Russ Loucks, Alix Magner, Cheryl Manley, Maggie Mansch, Kesha Marson, Sharon Marton-Thom, Desta Millner, Megan Morley, Shirley Muñoz Newson, Leslie Nagel, Lindsay Ness, Amy Ochs, Rob Ogren, Tina Olson, William O'Reilly, Kit Oslin, Jessi Peine, Cleve Pettersen, Brian Pinkowski, Sarah Pritzker, Kaveh Rahimi, Judy Ramaker, Mary Randleman, Aaron Reeves, Cori Reski, Spinner Reyerson, Marjorie Ryan, Alicia Salmos, Mary Sandell, Michele Schalin, Jonathan Senum, Victoria Servetas, Eli Shank, Katie Shoup, Maggie Smith, Abby Spilka, John "Jack" Stack, Dan Star, Heather Sterzinger, Nikki Sudberry, Ben Swenka, Morgan Sylvester, Morgan Sylvester, Lori Taylor, Lisa Thompson, Sherry Townsend, Alex Turner, Naomi Vladeck, Robin Voreis, Jamie Wagner, Denise Ward, Jill Wiehle, Robert Williams, Kaitlin Yilek, Sarah Young, Isaac Young, and Beth Yurchisin.

And to the amazingly brave visionaries who have shared their work, the work that filled my DIY recovery toolkit, I am forever grateful for your words. You inspire me more than you will ever know, and I owe so much of my growth to your brilliance.

Annie Grace, author of *This Naked Mind* and host of the affiliated podcast, captivated me immediately with the depth of her honesty and breadth of research she had done. Her words were the spark of change I needed to ignite my own triumphant return to myself.

Gabor Maté, M.D., author, physician, and addiction expert, speaks of addiction with such humanity and grace. It was the key to learning how to love myself. I've watched countless TED talks and interviews, always leaving more inspired than the last time. My copy of *In the Realm of Hungry Ghosts* is a little tattered and dogeared now, lovingly highlighted on near every page.

Authors Glennon Doyle and Melissa Febos inspired me to take a deeper look into the reasons behind so many dissonant parts of my life. Their authenticity and wisdom helped me embrace my inner voice and bring her into the light. Both *Untamed* and *Girlhood* have forever changed me in the most magical ways.

More amazing toolkit contributors I wouldn't be here without:
- Brené Brown Ph.D., L.M.S.W. - *The Gifts of Imperfection* & *Atlas of the Heart,* and her infamous TED talk on vulnerability
- Deepak Chopra - virtual fireside chat
- Carol S. Dweck, PhD - *Mindset*
- Sarah Hepola - *Blackout: Remembering the Things I Drank to Forget*
- Rachel Hollis - *Girl, Stop Apologizing* & *Start Today Journal*
- Laura McKowen - *We Are the Luckiest*
- Oriah Mountain Dreamer - *The Invitation*

Appendix

INTRO

"Myths About Drowning and Water Safety." 2018. Stop Drowning Now. Accessed January 15, 2023. https://www.stopdrowningnow.org/myths-about-drowning-and-water-safety.

National Institute on Alcohol Abuse and Alcoholism. 2020. "Understanding Alcohol Use Disorder." www.niaaa.nih.gov. Accessed February 16, 2023. https://www.niaaa.nih.gov/publications/brochures-and-fact-sheets/understanding-alcohol-use-disorder.

THE SENTENCE

Maté, Gabor MD. 2020. *In the Realm of Hungry Ghosts: Close Encounters with Addiction*. California: North Atlantic Books.

WOODLAKE LODGE

Di Chiara, M.D., Gaetano. 1997. "Alcohol and Dopamine". *Alcohol Health Research World* 21, 2: 108-114.

National Institute for Alcohol Abuse and Alcoholism. 2022. "Underage Drinking." www.niaaa.nih.gov. Accessed January 21, 2023. https://www.niaaa.nih.gov/publications/brochures-and-fact-sheets/underage-drinking.

Schultz, Wolfram. "Getting Formal with Dopamine and Reward". *Neuron* 2002; 36: 241–63. https://pubmed.ncbi.nlm.nih.gov/12383780/.

Schick MR, Nalven T, Spillane NS. 2022. "Drinking to Fit in: The Effects of Drinking Motives and Self-Esteem on Alcohol Use among Female College Students." *Substance Use Misuse* 57, no.1: 76-85.

Volkow, M.D., Nora D. and George F. Koob, Ph.D., and A. Thomas McLellan, Ph.D. 2016. "Neurobiologic Advances from the Brain Disease Model of Addiction." *New England Journal Medicine* 374, no. 4 (January 2016): 363–371.

GIRLS WHO WEAR NAIL POLISH

Maté, Gabor, MD. 2021. "The Power of Addiction and the Addiction to Power." Filmed October 2021 in Rio. TEDx video. 18:46. https://www.youtube.com/watch?v=66cYc-Sak6nE.

National Center on Domestic and Sexual Violence. 2004.
"Spousal Rape Laws: 20 Years Later." http://www.ncdsv.org/
images/NCVC_SpousalRapeLaws20YearsLater_2004.pdf.

CAMOUFLAGE

Eisenberger, N., Lieberman, M., Williams, K. 2003. "Does Rejection Hurt? An fMRI Study of Social Exclusion." *Science* 302, no. 5643 (November 2003): 290-2.

WHO, ME?

National Institute on Alcohol Abuse and Alcoholism.
2021. "Interrupted Memories: Alcohol-Induced Blackouts." National Institute on Alcohol Abuse and Alcoholism. Accessed September 7, 2022. https://www.niaaa.nih.gov/publications/brochures-and-fact-sheets/interrupted-memories-alcohol-induced-blackouts.

NOT 'ROCK BOTTOM' ENOUGH

Bellows, Alan. 2006. "The Most Boring Story Ever Told." Damn Interesting. Accessed January 22, 2023. https://www.damn-interesting.com/the-deepest-hole/.

Wilson, Bill. 2001. *Alcoholics Anonymous.* New York: Simon & Schuster.

Wilson, Bill. 2021. *The Twelve Steps and Twelve Traditions.* New York: Simon & Schuster.

PEDESTAL

National Institute on Alcohol Abuse and Alcoholism. 1995. "Alcohol Alert." National Institute on Alcohol Abuse and Alcoholism. No. 28 PH 356. April 1995. Accessed September 12, 2022. https://pubs.niaaa.nih.gov/publications/aa28.htm.

Scaccia, Annamarya. 2023. "Understanding Why Blackouts Happen." *Healthline.com,* updated January 22, 2023. https://www.healthline.com/health/what-causes-blackouts.

EYE OF THE HURRICANE

"The Eye."2020. *University of Illinois at Urbana-Champaign WW2010.* Accessed September 20, 2022. http://ww2010.atmos.uiuc.edu/(Gh)/guides/mtr/hurr/stages/cane/eye.rxml/.

"Hurricane Structure." 2020. *HurricaneScience.org.* Accessed September 20, 2022. http://www.hurricanescience.org/science/science/hurricanestructure/.

Pompili, Maurizio et al. 2010. "Suicidal Behavior and Alcohol Abuse." *International Journal of Environmental Research and Public Health* 7, no. 4: 1392-431. doi:10.3390/ijerph7041392. https://www.ncbi.nlm.nih.gov/pmc/articles/PMC2872355/#!po=0.381679. Accessed February 11, 2023.

THE GHOST OF KRISTY'S YET TO COME

Grace, Annie. 2017. "Who is Annie Grace & What is a Naked Mind." *This Naked Mind Podcast.* Released September 19, 2017. Podcast, 34 min. https://thisnakedmind.libsyn.com/ep-01-who-is-annie-grace-what-is-a-naked-mind.

Grace, Annie. 2018. *This Naked Mind*. New York: Penguin Random House LLC.

Rose, Brian. 2019. "Gabor Maté - Childhood Trauma Creates Addiction." Filmed January 2019 in London. Video, 2:01:37. https://londonreal.tv/gabor-mate-childhood-trauma-creates-addiction/.

DON'T JUST RISE

Horne, John. n.d. "The Babe's Called Shot." National Baseball Hall of Fame. Accessed September 28, 2022. https://baseballhall.org/discover-more/stories/baseball-history/called-shot.

Mohr, Howard. 1987. *How to Talk Minnesotan: A Visitor's Guide*. New York: Penguin Group.

WAVES

White, Aaron PhD, Castle, I-Jen PhD, Powell, Patricia PhD, Hingson, Ralph ScD, Koob, George PhD. 2022. "Alcohol-Related Deaths During the COVID-19 Pandemic." *JAMA* 327, no. 17 (March 2022): 1704-1706. https://jamanetwork.com/journals/jama/fullarticle/2790491.

SURVIVING THE FIRES

Mullen, Luba. 2017."How Trees Survive and Thrive After A Fire." National Forest Foundation. Accessed September 16, 2022. https://www.nationalforests.org/our-forests/your-national-forests-magazine/how-trees-survive-and-thrive-after-a-fire.

XBONNEVILLE

Brown, Brené. 2021. *Atlas of the Heart*. New York: Random House.